W9-AXD-582

CULTURE SMART!
CAMBODIA

Graham Saunders

·K·U·P·E·R·A·R·D·

This book is available for special discounts for bulk purchases for sales promotions or premiums. Special editions, including personalized covers, excerpts of existing books, and corporate imprints, can be created in large quantities for special needs.

For more information in the USA write to Special Markets/Premium Sales, 1745 Broadway, MD 6–2, New York, NY 10019, or e-mail specialmarkets@randomhouse.com.

In the United Kingdom contact Kuperard publishers at the address below.

ISBN 978 1 85733 471 5
This book is also available as an e-book: eISBN 978 1 85733 602 3

British Library Cataloguing in Publication Data
A CIP catalogue entry for this book is available from the British Library

First published in Great Britain 2008
by Kuperard, an imprint of Bravo Ltd
59 Hutton Grove, London N12 8DS
Tel: +44 (0) 20 8446 2440 Fax: +44 (0) 20 8446 2441
www.culturesmart.co.uk
Inquiries: sales@kuperard.co.uk

Distributed in the United States and Canada
by Random House Distribution Services
1745 Broadway, New York, NY 10019
Tel: +1 (212) 572-2844 Fax: +1 (212) 572-4961
Inquiries: csorders@randomhouse.com

Series Editor Geoffrey Chesler
Design Bobby Birchall

Printed in Malaysia

Cover image: Angkor Wat at sunset. © *Pomortzeff/Dreamstime.com*
Images on pages 14 © Kabir Bakie, 16 and 98 © Oliver Spalt,
23 © Charles J. Sharp, 44 © James Hathaway, 49 © Colocho,
53 © sam garza, 57 © willposh, 63 © Thomas Wanhoff,
67 and 91 (bottom) © n ole, 75 © Jialing Gao, 80 © Thomas
Schoch, 81 © Cambodia4kids, 96 © Mat Connolley, 97 © Brett
Matthews, 104 © Calliopejen, 105 © Bernd Nottelmann, 108 © Erik
Hooymans, 118 and 140 © Dvtouch, 127 © Manfred Werner, and
131 © David Wilmot.

About the Author

GRAHAM SAUNDERS has a Ph.D in East Asian studies from the University of Hull, England. An Australian by birth, he spent twenty-eight years teaching in East Malaysia and Brunei, and has made numerous visits to the countries of the region, including Cambodia. He then taught in Cyprus for five years before he and his wife, Anne, settled in England, near York. After some part-time university lecturing he retired to run a business specializing in books on Southeast Asia. He is the author of a number of books and articles on the history of this area, including *Culture Smart! Indonesia.*

contents

Map of Cambodia	7
Introduction	8
Key Facts	10

CHAPTER 1: LAND AND PEOPLE | 12
- Geography | 12
- Climate | 14
- The People | 15
- A Brief History | 17
- The Economy | 34
- Government | 38

CHAPTER 2: VALUES AND ATTITUDES | 40
- Religion and Values | 40
- The Family | 44
- Attitudes to Time | 47
- Attitudes to Foreigners | 48
- Attitudes to Asian Neighbors | 49
- Attitudes to Minorities | 50

CHAPTER 3: RELIGION AND FESTIVALS | 52
- Religions of Cambodia | 52
- Festivals and National Celebrations | 55
- Public Holidays | 58
- Rites of Passage | 59

CHAPTER 4: MAKING FRIENDS | 66
- Social Behavior | 66
- Greetings | 66
- Dress | 68
- Invitations | 69

CHAPTER 5: THE CAMBODIANS AT HOME | 74
- Housing | 74
- Daily Life and Routine | 76

- The Family   79
- Education   82
- Entertaining   84
- Household Help   88

CHAPTER 6: TIME OUT   90
- Traditional Culture   90
- *Wats* and Pagodas   92
- Sports, Games, and Other Entertainments   93
- Food and Drink   94
- Eating Out   97
- Bars and Nightclubs   99
- Photography   100
- Shopping for Pleasure   100

CHAPTER 7: TRAVEL, HEALTH, AND SAFETY   106
- Arrival   106
- Travel Within the Country   107
- Health and Medical Care   112
- Safety   115
- Places to Visit   116
- The Temple Complex of Angkor   124

CHAPTER 8: BUSINESS BRIEFING   140
- Government Policy   140
- Business Culture   142
- Office Etiquette and Protocol   143
- Management Style   144
- Business Cards   144
- Meetings and Greetings   145
- Negotiations   147
- Speeches and Presentations   148
- Bureaucracy and Corruption   149
- Gift Giving   150
- Women in Business   151

contents

- Working within the System   152
- Blessing the Project   152

CHAPTER 9: COMMUNICATING   154
- Language   154
- Face-to-Face   156
- Humor   157
- Body Language   158
- Services   160
- The Media   161
- Conclusion   162

Appendix: Useful Words and Phrases   163
Further Reading   165
Index   166
Acknowledgment   168

Map of Cambodia

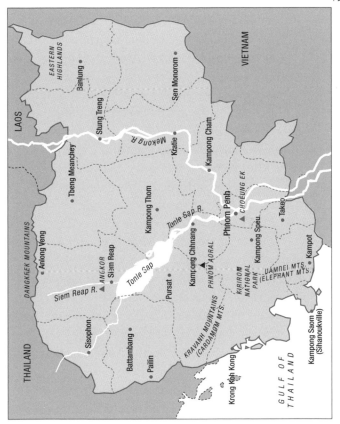

introduction

Say "Cambodia," and two associations come to mind: the lost glories of Angkor, and the horrors of the Khmer Rouge's "Killing Fields." Any understanding of Cambodia today must embrace both these opposites, as well as the changing attitudes caused by a demographic revolution.

Cambodia was the center of the Khmer empire, which from its capital at Angkor from the ninth to the fourteenth centuries ruled much of what is now Vietnam, Laos, and Thailand. The ruins of the Khmers' palaces, temples, and cities testify to their power, wealth, high culture, and engineering skills, and their abandonment and long obscurity provide a sobering example of civilization's fragility. That one of the world's great civilizations arose here and left a heritage of such power and beauty is a source of great pride for Cambodians.

After the Thais captured Angkor in 1431, the Khmers moved their capital to Phnom Penh and maintained a precarious independence—a situation exploited by Portugal and Spain, until the expulsion of the Spanish in 1599. From 1600 the Thais and the Vietnamese vied for influence over Cambodia, beset as it was by rivalry within the royal family. In 1863 the French established themselves in Phnom Penh and brought

Cambodia increasingly under their control. While retaining the trappings of monarchy, it became virtually a French colony.

During the Second World War, the Japanese occupation demolished French prestige. After the war, Cambodian opposition and the conflict in Vietnam rendered the French position untenable, and in 1953 King Sihanouk declared Cambodia's independence, but the troubled years that followed culminated in the brutal regime of Pol Pot and the Khmer Rouge. In the 1970s an estimated one and a half million people were killed by execution, starvation, or forced labor. Those who have survived carry with them memories and guilt. Young people, however, know only what they may have heard from their families: the subject is not openly discussed.

Thankfully, Cambodia today has reentered the world community. Tourism thrives. Visitors are surprised by the resilience of its people. Culturally they share many of the values of their neighbors, influenced by the faiths and cultures of India and China but possessing distinctive languages, styles, and customs of their own. Despite the traumatic past, Cambodians remain courteous, hospitable, good-natured, and welcoming to visitors.

Key Facts

Official Name	Kingdom of Cambodia	Preah Reacheanachakr Kampuchea
Capital City	Phnom Penh	Pop. 2 million approx.
Other Cities and Towns	Battambang; Kampot; Kampong Cham; Siem Reap; Kampong Saom (Sihanoukville); Kampong Thom; Sisophon; Takeo	
Area	69,990 sq. miles (181,040 sq. km), of which land 68,154 sq. miles (176,519 sq. km)	
Climate	Tropical. Wet monsoon season (May to October); dry season (November to March). Hot and humid; more moderate in the highlands.	Temperatures range from the high 70s°F (20s°C) in the cool season (December to January) to the high 90s°F (30s°C) in the hot season (April to May).
Population	14 million approx.	Growth rate: 1.73%
Ethnic Makeup	Khmer 90%; Vietnamese 5% ; Chinese 1%; others 4%	
Age Structure	0–14 years 34%; 15–64 years 62.4%; 65 years and above 3.6% (2007 estimates)	
Birthrate	25.53/1000; death rate 8.24/1000 (2007 estimates)	

Language	Khmer	English and French are widely spoken
Adult Literacy	Approx. 74%	
Religion	Theravada Buddhism 95%; others (Christian, Muslim, animist) 5%	
Government	Multiparty democracy under a constitutional monarchy	Bicameral parliament consisting of the National Assembly and the Senate. Members of both houses serve 5-year terms.
Currency	The riel. 1 riel=100 sen	US dollars accepted. Thai Baht accepted in west of country
Media	Seven TV stations, plus two relay stations for French and Vietnamese broadcasts	Khmer newspapers: *Reaksmei Kampuchea*, *Kaoh Santepheap*. English-language newspapers: *Cambodia Daily*, *Phnom Penh Post*
Electricity	220 volts, 50 Hz	Flat or round 2-pronged plugs
Video/TV	NTSC system	
Internet Domain	.kh	
Telephone	The international dialing code is 855.	The code for Phnom Penh is 23.
Time Zone	GMT + 7 hours	

chapter one

LAND & PEOPLE

GEOGRAPHY

Situated on the Indochinese peninsula, Cambodia is bordered by Thailand on the west, Thailand and Laos on the north, Vietnam on the east, and the Gulf of Thailand, with a 274-mile (443-km) coastline, on the southwest. The Mekong River flows through eastern Cambodia from Laos in the north. At Phnom Penh, the capital, it divides into two courses, which exit through southern Vietnam to the South China Sea. To the northwest of Phnom Penh is the vast Tonle Sap Lake, linked to Phnom Penh and the Mekong by a sixty-two-mile (100-km) channel known as the Tonle Sap River. When the Mekong rises during the rainy season from May to October, water flows northwest from the Mekong to the Tonle Sap Lake, which expands in area from 1,865 square miles (3,000 sq. km) to more than 4,350 square miles (7,500 sq. km), and in depth from a little over 6 feet (2 m) to 33 feet (10 m). During the dry season, as the Mekong lowers, the water flows from the lake back to the Mekong. For centuries this phenomenon has created the great, low-lying alluvial plain upon which most Cambodians live. Surrounding this is a large area of slightly higher plain rising to about 330 feet (100 m), which supports woodland and grassland. Beyond this the country is bounded by high land: the Cardamom Mountains and the Elephant Mountains in the southwest, which include Cambodia's highest peak, Phnom Aoral (6,003 feet; 1,830 m); the Dangrek Mountains along the northern border with Thailand, marked by an east-west escarpment, 186 miles (300 km) long and rising 590 feet to 1,640 feet (180 to 500 m) from the plain; the Eastern Highlands in the northeast; to the west, highland separates the densely wooded coastal strip from the plain of the interior.

The Environment
The central plain has been cultivated for centuries, growing irrigated rice, a variety of fruits, corn, and tobacco. Beyond the irrigated areas the plain supports tall savanna-style grassland and woodland. The Eastern Highlands

have both grasslands and deciduous forests. The highlands of the north and southwest have forests, ranging from tropical rain forest on the southwestern slopes to pine forests at higher altitudes. The coastal strip has lowland evergreen forest on higher ground and mangroves along the coast. The forested areas support many varieties of orchids. However, in recent decades these forest habitats have become threatened by logging.

Logging also threatens the native fauna, including the rhinoceros, tiger, leopard, and wild

ox. Elephants are less endangered because of their utility, although they are threatened in the wild. There is a wide variety of butterflies and birds. Visitors will mainly be aware of the waterbirds inhabiting the region of the Tonle Sap and the shores of the Mekong. There are four types of poisonous snake: the cobra, the king cobra, the banded krait, and the Russell's viper.

CLIMATE

Cambodia's climate is tropical, and governed by monsoons: the cool, dry, northeast monsoon from November to March and the warm, wet, southwest monsoon from May to early October, bringing strong winds and heavy rain. However, not all days

are wet, and the rain, when it falls, usually comes
in the afternoons. The interval between monsoons
tends to be variable. Annual rainfall varies from
about 200 inches (5,000 mm) on the slopes of
the southwestern highlands to about 60 inches
(1,400 mm) in the central plain. The average
temperatures in the country range from around
82°F (28°C) in January to 91°F (33°C) or more in
April. Phnom Penh is perhaps best visited in the
December to February period, when humidity is
low and it is relatively cool, with little rain.
Temperatures rise from early February, and can
reach a peak of more than 104°F (40°C) in April.

THE PEOPLE

The population is 90 percent Khmer, 5 percent
Vietnamese, and 1 percent Chinese, other ethnic
groups making up the remaining 4 percent.

The Khmer were the original inhabitants of the
flat, low-lying lands of the Mekong Basin. They
practice Theravada Buddhism, and their language
is the official language of the country, spoken by
95 percent of the population. (Many people in the
urban and tourist areas speak English and
French.) The Vietnamese immigrated at different
times during French colonial rule, some as minor
officials and clerks in the colonial bureaucracy,
others as laborers on the rubber plantations.
Many were expelled by the Pol Pot regime and
returned when Vietnamese forces overthrew the
Khmer Rouge. Most have settled as rice farmers

near the Vietnamese border, and there is a Vietnamese fishing community on the Tonle Sap Lake. Generally, they are among the less well-off in the population. The Chinese are mainly urban, and are occupied in commerce, banking, and trade. They also suffered under the Khmer Rouge, but their expertise and connections have helped them prosper in recent years as commerce and industry are again encouraged. The remaining 4 percent of the population comprises the Khmer Loeu, also known as the Chuenchet, highland tribal peoples who live as subsistence farmers and hunter-gatherers in the forested mountains of the northeast, and the Chams, a Muslim minority who came from the border region with Vietnam and whose ancestors once fought the Khmers and captured Angkor. Their language is related to Malay; they converted to Islam in the fourteenth century, and adopted Islamic dress. They are to be found throughout Cambodia but are concentrated in Kampong Cham, northeast of Phnom Penh.

The overall literacy rate is about 74 percent: 85 percent for men and 60 percent for women. Life expectancy is roughly fifty-nine years for men and sixty-three years for women. More than 50 percent of the population is under twenty-one.

A BRIEF HISTORY

Archaeological research indicates that by 1000 BCE the inhabitants of the region were living much as they do today, in houses on stilts and eating rice and fish. The Mekong Basin was fertile and could support a large population—those whom we now know as the Khmer, who had their own language and prospered as farmers—while the Mekong River gave access to the sea and to the fertile delta region. The different peoples began to coalesce into larger communities based on agriculture, crafts, and trade. As the population increased and trade and prosperity grew, so political centers developed and expanded to encompass weaker neighbors. The region became a transit for trade between India and China, while from India came first Hinduism, around the first century CE, and then Buddhism, replacing or subsuming the animistic beliefs of the original inhabitants and introducing changes in lifestyle and ideas.

Early Kingdoms

The first major state to emerge in the region was Funan, based in the Mekong Delta and lasting from the first to the sixth centuries CE. Much of the culture and many of the political institutions of succeeding Khmer states were derived from Funan. Funan itself was subsequently absorbed into the new state of Chenla, which had broken away from Funan in the mid-sixth century. In the late seventh century, Chenla divided into north and south (Land Chenla and Water Chenla).

Water Chenla had widespread maritime trade, reaching as far as modern Indonesia, but it was politically unstable and may have suffered a Javanese invasion. In troubled times it was possible for an ambitious and capable man to establish himself as a political leader and dream of establishing his own minor kingdom. By the end of the eighth century CE a Khmer kingdom had been established near the Tonle Sap Lake, and in 802 CE began that prolonged period of Khmer political predominance and cultural splendor that came to an end only with the sacking of Angkor by the Thais in 1431.

The Khmer Empire

The ruler who inaugurated this period of Khmer predominance was Jayavarman II (802–50), who claimed descent from earlier rulers and had returned from exile in Java. On assuming power, and drawing on Hindu precedents, Jayavarman II instituted a new state religion with himself as *devaraja*, or god-king. During his reign, he established himself at four capitals around the Tonle Sap, the last of which was eight miles (13 km) from modern Siem Reap. Jayavarman II's new politico-religious system bolstered the ruler's prestige, power, and right to rule and demand obedience from his subjects. His nephew, Indravarman I (877–89), laid the economic foundations for Angkor's wealth and growth with a feat of hydraulic engineering remarkable for its size and precision and making possible the irrigation and cultivation of large areas of land, extended even further by his successors, capable of supporting a large population in a relatively small area and providing the wealth and manpower for the emerging Khmer empire. Indravarman's successor, Yasovarman (889–910), seeking a site on which to celebrate his own glory and prestige, moved the capital to the Angkor area, where it was to remain until the mid-fifteenth century.

The religion of the early Angkorian state was Hinduism, and the influence of southern India is evident in its architecture, sculpture, and political organization. Hinduism had flourished in the region for several centuries, and was represented by the worship of Shiva and Vishnu embodied in a single deity known as Marinara. At the time of the move to Angkor, Shiva was the deity favored by the king, to be replaced in the twelfth century by Vishnu. The temples and shrines at Angkor are reflections in stone of Hindu cosmology, the central towers being representations of Mount

Meru, the home of the gods. Buddhism had also entered Cambodia by the first century CE and had coexisted with Hinduism, but it was not embraced by its rulers until the thirteenth century.

The Rise of Theravada Buddhism

During the thirteenth century, Hinduism gave way to Theravada Buddhism as the state religion, with Pali replacing Sanskrit as the sacred language at the beginning of the fourteenth century.

There are two major schools of Buddhism, known as the Theravada (Teaching of the Elders) School and the Mahayana (Great Vehicle) School. Theravada Buddhists regard their form as purer, reflecting more accurately the teachings of the Buddha. This form of Buddhism entered Cambodia through Southeast Asia from Southern India (it is often referred to as the "southern school"), whereas Mahayana Buddhism (also referred to as the "northern school") was carried through Nepal, Tibet, and China to Vietnam, and acquired accretions and practices that the Theravada Buddhists reject. Mayayana Buddhists refer to the Theravada school as the Hinayana (lesser vehicle), because of its more austere doctrine and practices.

The Decline of the Khmers

Over the following two centuries, Angkor fought wars against its Thai, Vietnamese, and Cham neighbors, the latter living in the area of south-central Vietnam. Fortunes wavered. The Chams, for example, defeated in the early twelfth century, rallied and inflicted a major defeat on the Khmers and occupied and sacked Angkor itself. They could not maintain their supremacy and were in turn defeated by Jayavarman VII (1181–1211), who built the new city of Angkor Thom, upon

the walls of which the exploits of the king, including his defeat of the Chams on the Tonle Sap Lake, are vividly inscribed.

Over the next two hundred years, Khmer power slowly declined, partly because incursions by the Thais damaged the delicately balanced irrigation system. Consequently the capital was moved to Phnom Penh in the mid-fifteenth century, after the Thais had once again captured Angkor. During the following century and a half, the kingdom was weakened internally by dynastic rivalry and constantly threatened by the Thais to the west and, to a lesser extent, by the Vietnamese.

By this time, the European powers were showing interest in the region. Spain established a presence in 1593, at first at the invitation of the king. This ended with the massacre of the Spanish garrison at Phnom Penh in 1599. Thereafter, a series of weak kings sought assistance against their dynastic rivals by allying themselves with either Thailand or Vietnam, until in 1863 King Norodom (1860–1904) signed an agreement making Cambodia a French protectorate.

In the 1860s France had acquired Cochin-China (southern Vietnam) as a colony. In 1884, it established protectorates over Annam and Tonkin (central and northern Vietnam). Finally, in 1887 it created the Union of Indochina, combining the four states under the overall authority of a Governor General. Laos was added in 1893.

THE "DISCOVERY" OF ANGKOR WAT

The French naturalist and explorer Henri Mouhot (1826–61) made four expeditions to the inner regions of Indochina, on the last of which he died, on November 10, 1861, in Laos. His diaries were returned to his wife, and were published three times in quick succession. They appeared first in French, in magazine form, in 1863. In 1864 they were published in English in book form as *Travels in the Central Parts of Indo-china (Siam), Cambodia and Laos.* A French book edition was published in 1868. All these had engraved illustrations, many based on Mouhot's own drawings. A few European travelers had visited Angkor before, and had written of it, but Mouhot's more detailed account and illustrations evoked a new interest, particularly in England and France. The time, also, was ripe: the 1860s were witnessing a period of European imperial expansion, accompanied by intellectual curiosity and scientific research.

Mouhot's collection of specimens and descriptions of natural life were his principal interest. Nevertheless, he felt compelled to describe to the world Angkor, its ruins, and the civilization that it represented, and spoke of Angkor Wat as a temple to "rival that of Solomon, and erected by some ancient Michael Angelo," and as "grander than anything left to us by Greece or Rome," presenting "a sad contrast to the state of barbarism in which the nation is now plunged." But there was also another, more material, enticement to attract European attention: "Neither must I omit to mention the various productions which form so important a part of the riches of a nation, and which might be here cultivated in the greatest perfection. I would especially instance cotton,

coffee, indigo, tobacco, and the mulberry, and such spices as nutmegs, cloves and ginger— What might not be accomplished if these were colonies . . . governed as the dependencies of a great and generous nation." When the time came, that nation would be French; but Mouhot had brought Angkor into public consciousness in Europe, and that consciousness identified Cambodia as the home of Angkor—an identification that has persisted to the present and has become the basis of the Cambodian tourist industry.

French Control

At first the French protectorate had little impact
on Cambodia's internal affairs, except to check
further incursions from Thailand and Vietnam and
protect King Norodom from his rivals. In 1870,
however, the French forced King Norodom to sign
a treaty that made Cambodia a French colony in
all but name. This provoked a rebellion that lasted
two years, until the French agreed to revert to the
pre-treaty situation. French control was gradually
reasserted by agreement with Cambodian officials
who saw advantages in acquiescing. In return the
court was retained in splendor as the symbol of
Cambodian sovereignty, and French pressure
upon Thailand brought about the return of the
northwestern provinces of Battambang and
Siem Reap and the town of Sisophon to Cambodia
in 1907. Thus Angkor was again Cambodian. King
Norodom was succeeded by Kings Sisowath
(1904–27) and Monivong (1927–41). By the time
of the latter's death, the Japanese had occupied
French Indochina.

Japanese Occupation

As servants of the wartime French Vichy government, the French colonial authorities remained in place and the French Governor General placed the eighteen-year-old Prince Sihanouk upon the throne. However, under pressure from the Japanese, the French authorities returned most of Battambang and Siem Reap provinces to Thailand, which did not return them to Cambodian control until 1947. After the

fall of the Vichy government in Paris toward the end of the war in Europe, the Japanese assumed control of the government of Cambodia, jailing the French administrators, until Japan itself surrendered and the French returned. The war period saw a great decline in French prestige and an increase in Khmer national feeling.

Guerrilla War and Independence

After the defeat of Japan, Cambodia was granted autonomy within the French Union, but the return to colonial rule was resented. Cambodian Communists, influenced by the Viet Minh insurrection in Vietnam, began an armed resistance in the areas bordering Vietnam, while the Thais provided some assistance to Cambodian rebels on their border. The Khmer Issarak (Free

Khmer) were little more than bands of guerrilla
fighters, but the French were overstretched in
Vietnam. They had cloaked their control of
Cambodia with the splendour of the royal court,
thus enabling King Sihanouk to rally Khmer
national feeling around the monarchy.

Facing opposition to his role from the
Democratic Party in Cambodia, King Sihanouk
dissolved the Cambodian parliament in January
1953, declared martial law, and canvassed
international support for full Cambodian
independence, which he proclaimed in November
1953 and which was ratified by the Geneva
Conference of May 1954 as part of the
international agreements on Indochina.

In order to play a more active political role free
of the restraints of monarchy, Sihanouk abdicated
in favor of his father, Norodom Suramarit, in
March 1955 and created his own political party. In
the elections of September 1955, Sihanouk's
People's Socialist Community (Sangkum Reastr
Niyum) won every seat in parliament, giving him
a democratic mandate. Sihanouk was prime
minister until his father's death in 1960, and
thenceforth became head of state, retaining the
title of Prince. Suspicious of the policies of the
United States, which supported Thailand and
South Vietnam, both of whom he distrusted,
Sihanouk declared Cambodia neutral in
international affairs. In May 1965, perceiving
plots against him by the United States, he broke
off diplomatic relations with Washington and

inclined toward Vietnam and China, turning a blind eye to North Vietnamese and Vietcong use of Cambodian territory as a sanctuary and supply route for their forces in their conflict with South Vietnam and the United States.

The Cambodian Civil War

Sihanouk's foreign and domestic policies alienated both right and left wings of the Cambodian political field. The urban elite and the officer corps opposed his socialist economic policies and his foreign policy, while many left-leaning educated Cambodians resented the suppression of political dissent. Widespread corruption was resented by all classes, although Sihanouk himself enjoyed a semidivine status in the eyes of most of the population. A Maoist-inspired rural rebellion in 1967 caused Sihanouk to turn against the left. In 1968 the United States began bombing inside Cambodian territory to destroy Communist bases and disrupt their supply lines, the Ho Chi Minh trail. These operations developed into a carpet-bombing campaign that killed thousands of Cambodian peasants, created a major refugee problem, and turned more of the peasantry against the Americans and toward the Communists.

The Overthrow of Sihanouk

The conflict between the army and the rebels within Cambodia worsened, while Sihanouk's policy of neutrality had cut Cambodia off from

United States aid, and his government's policy of nationalization alienated the middle classes and banking and commercial communities. While Sihanouk was abroad in March 1970, the pro-Western General Lon Nol and Prince Sisowath Matak deposed him and established the Khmer Republic. Sihanouk set up a government-in-exile in Beijing. The political coalition he headed included a Cambodian revolutionary movement known as the Khmer Rouge, to which many Sihanouk supporters opposed to Lon Nol turned. Civil war broke out between the Khmer National Armed Forces (FANK) and the Cambodian People's National Liberation Armed Forces, which soon fell under the control of the Khmer Rouge.

In April 1970, US and South Vietnamese forces invaded Cambodia in an attempt to expel the North Vietnamese from their bases, causing the North Vietnamese and Vietcong forces to retreat further into the country, increasing the threat to Lon Nol, whose corrupt government was already unpopular. Chaos was unleashed as fighting erupted throughout the countryside and the US bombing campaign continued (it ended only in August 1973), killing thousands and driving thousands more into Phnom Penh and other cities. The result was a surge of support for the Khmer Rouge.

Rise of the Khmer Rouge

Over this period, the Khmer Rouge, which had originally taken refuge in the countryside to escape Sihanouk's security forces, emerged as a dominant force under the leadership of Pol Pot (Saloth Sar) and Khieu Samphan. Lon Nol was regarded as a  threat by the North Vietnamese, who had benefited from Sihanouk's neutrality and reluctance to oppose them, and saw in the Khmer Rouge a force to be encouraged in opposition to Lon Nol. North Vietnamese forces entered northeast Cambodia, pushed out Lon Nol's troops, and provided training and arms to the Khmer Rouge, making them an effective military force. The most ideological, disciplined, and ruthless of the forces resisting the Lon Nol regime, they extended their dominance over other Cambodian opponents of it, including supporters of Sihanouk and those left-wing and Communist elements influenced by North Vietnam or the Vietcong. As they recruited and indoctrinated fresh forces from the disaffected peasantry, the Khmer Rouge began a purge of those whom they distrusted, including those Cambodians who had received training in North Vietnam and those whom they suspected of attachment to Sihanouk. By early 1975, the Khmer Rouge was in control of the countryside and Phnom Penh was virtually isolated.

THE KHMER ROUGE

The term "Khmer Rouge" ("Red Cambodian") was first used by Prince Norodom Sihanouk in the 1960s to differentiate this left-wing Communist movement from the right-wing "Khmer Bleu." Its leaders had become Marxists as students in Paris in the 1950s, and had joined the French Communist party. They had also acquired the intellectualism of revolutionary France and a belief that ideals could be realized if pursued and implemented with ruthless clarity. To bring about the ideal, in this case the creation of a Communist peasant farming society, any action was permissible.

This was an ideology and mind-set alien to Cambodian social culture; yet perhaps there were some parallels with those absolute Angkorian monarchs of old who drove their people to great achievements.

The Reign of Terror

In April 1975, Lon Nol fled. The Khmer Rouge seized Phnom Penh and immediately introduced a radical agrarian revolution. In an attempt to completely restructure Cambodian society, they began a ruthless extermination of all possible opponents of their dream to build a Maoist, peasant-dominated, agrarian society. The cities were emptied, and some two million people, mainly

from the educated and middle classes, were systematically killed. Sihanouk, the nominal head of state, was removed from power. Cut off almost entirely from the outside world, Cambodia, now named Democratic Kampuchea, became a slave state.

Vietnamese Invasion

In December 1978, responding to Cambodian incursions across their borders, the Vietnamese, in the name of the Kampuchean United Front for National Salvation, invaded and forced the remnants of the Khmer Rouge back to the jungles on the Thai border. Cambodia was renamed The People's Republic of Kampuchea and gained a new anti-Pol Pot Communist government (PRK) headed by Heng Samrin. The country slowly began to rebuild itself under Vietnamese protection.

In the international climate of the day, the Vietnamese action did not meet with universal approval. The Soviet Union had supported the Vietnamese, but the Khmer Rouge in their Thailand refuge now received military aid from China. Royalist and republican groups also emerged. In June 1982 a coalition of all anti-Vietnamese factions was brought together under the auspices of the Association of Southeast Asian

Nations (ASEAN) to create what was called the Coalition Government of Democratic Kampuchea to challenge the Vietnamese-backed regime in Phnom Penh. The coalition included the Khmer Rouge. Faced with economic problems and the withdrawal of Soviet support, Vietnam withdrew its main forces in 1989.

Ceasefire and the UN Peace Process
In October 1991, an International Conference on Cambodia reached an accord whereby the United Nations would take responsibility for implementing a peace plan leading to free general elections in 1993. In the interim, the different factions agreed to establish a Supreme National Council, under Prince Sihanouk's chairmanship, which would formally delegate powers to the United Nations Transitional Authority in Cambodia (UNTAC), including a supervisory role

in administration and responsibilities for peacekeeping and conducting elections. The Khmer Rouge did not cooperate with UNTAC, refusing to disarm and stand down their forces or to permit access to their areas of control. On the other side, there was some intimidation by the government in Phnom Penh of a popular political faction led by Prince Sihanouk's eldest son, Prince Ranariddh. Despite tensions and fears of violence and a Khmer Rouge call for a boycott, the elections went ahead during May 23–29 and were peaceful. There was a 90 percent turnout of the 4.6 million registered voters for the elections, which the United Nations Security Council deemed free and fair.

The Khmer Rouge had boycotted the elections, and elements in the army aided their resistance to the new government—an unstable coalition of Prince Ranariddh's National United Front for an Independent, Neutral, Peaceful and Cooperative Cambodia (FUNCINPEC) and Hun Sen's Cambodian People's Party (CPP).

The New Constitution
The elections enabled the drafting of a new constitution and the restoration of Norodom Sihanouk as constitutional monarch. A government amnesty encouraged defections from the Khmer Rouge, which increased when the movement was outlawed in mid-1994. The coalition collapsed in violence in July 1997. Hun Sen emerged as sole leader, a position confirmed

by the elections in mid-1998, despite complaints about electoral malpractice. Pol Pot died in April 1998, before he could be brought to trial, and the UN abandoned other war crime trials because of doubts about the integrity of the courts.

The Cambodian People's Party won the elections in 2003, but did not find a coalition partner until June 2004. King Norodom Sihanouk abdicated in favor of his son, King Sihamoni, in October 2005. During 2006 Hun Sen reached a

level of reconciliation with opposition leader Sam Rainsy of the Royalist party, FUNCINPEC, which was riven by infighting. The elections due in July 2008 will determine whether the Cambodian People's Party can remain in power. Despite Hun Sen's tendency to strong-arm tactics, he has provided an element of stability that has in recent years seen some revival of Cambodia's economy and of foreign investment.

THE ECONOMY

For centuries, Cambodia's economy has been based on agriculture, with about 85 percent of the cultivated land devoted to growing rice and much of the rest to rubber. Fishing is also of major importance, much of it based on the Tonle Sap, and there is some breeding of cattle. The upheavals of the early 1970s caused a dramatic decline in production, and Cambodia required aid from the United States. Faced with this situation on coming to power, the Khmer Rouge regime, for ideological and political reasons, determined to make Cambodia self-sufficient. Thus began the forced exodus from the cities and towns to provide labor for rice cultivation and large-scale irrigation projects. Private ownership of land was disallowed, all land was transferred to the state or to state-run cooperatives, and industry was nationalized. The dispossession and execution of the educated and skilled classes removed just those people with the skills necessary to carry out and supervise the government's schemes. The disruption was considerable, and food was rationed and distributed by the state.

The Vietnamese-backed government of the People's Republic of Kampuchea, which took over in 1979, inherited a very battered economy requiring considerable reconstruction. Much of the infrastructure had been damaged or destroyed and famine was only averted with international food aid. As late as 1986, the government had to appeal to international agencies for rice. Nevertheless, by the mid-1980s the economy had returned to its healthy pre-1975 level, though there was still much to do in terms of reconstruction and attracting investment.

In 1989 the new anti-Vietnamese coalition government began to reverse the socialist policies it had inherited. Legislation was passed to restore the right to own and inherit property, denationalization began, and private enterprise was encouraged. A liberal investment code was introduced, the official currency rate was decontrolled, and restrictions on foreign trade were lifted. The impact of these reforms was felt first in Phnom Penh and the towns, and did not impinge greatly upon the 80 percent of workers employed in agriculture, especially as one consequence was rising inflation. Attempts to stabilize the riel did not succeed until 1994, after a period when it had been withdrawn from circulation.

Economic reform and recovery was hastened by the presence of the UNTAC in the period 1991–93. The 22,000 United Nations personnel stationed in the country created a demand for consumer goods, which stimulated trade and investment—a situation helped further by America's lifting of its trade embargo against Cambodia in January 1994.

The elections of 1993 brought FUNCINPEC into government, where it acquired the financial and economic portfolios. National budget and

financial structure laws established central control of the economy, and tax, investment, banking, and currency laws were reformed and liberalized to encourage foreign investment, and to provide both protection against nationalization and guarantees of equal treatment with nationals, except in land ownership. Over the next few years economic growth and levels of inflation fluctuated in response to external factors, but the overall trend was positive. The Asian financial crisis of 1998 combined with drought and internal political unrest caused problems, but Cambodia's admission to the Association of Southeast Asian Nations (ASEAN) in 1999 marked its full entry as a partner in the region.

The manufacturing side of the economy was led by textiles. Despite the expiration in January 2005 of a World Trade Organization agreement that had protected the Cambodian textile industry from direct competition with lower-cost Chinese and Indian production, textiles grew by 13 percent in 2006, with the government committing itself to high labor standards.

Between 2001 and 2004 the economy grew at an average rate of 6.4 percent, with tourism playing an increasingly important role. In 2005 tourist numbers exceeded one million for the first time, and numbers continue to increase.

Cambodia has a wide range of minerals, including gold, bauxite, copper, tin, and zinc, along with granite and silicone sand. Since 2005 the government has encouraged foreign investment, with Australian mining companies showing particular interest and setting up joint venture projects to carry out exploration. In addition, the discovery of offshore oil and natural gas resources by the US company Chevron offers the prospect of oil production beginning in 2011.

In the northeast, where mining activity has expanded, there is also hope that timber extraction will be conducted in a more sustainable way and that illegal logging can be controlled. However, there is concern that the exploitation of resources will have a detrimental effect on Cambodia's forests and cultivable land, although the government expresses awareness of these concerns.

A major problem for the economy is the legacy of the thirty years of war and repression when a generation was lost to education and training. We have seen that more than half the population are below the age of twenty-one. There is a shortage of skills, particularly in the countryside, and a lack of basic infrastructure. The problem for the government is to encourage the private sector to address this imbalance in cooperation with bilateral and multilateral donors such as the World Bank and the IMF. The imbalances may be gauged by the fact that agriculture employs 75 percent of the workforce but provides only 35.1 percent of GNP, while industry provides 26.2 percent of GNP and the service industries 38.6 percent, reflecting the importance of tourism in the economy.

GOVERNMENT

Cambodia is a multiparty liberal democracy under a constitutional monarchy. The monarch is head of state and is chosen by the Royal Throne Council; the present monarch is King Norodom Sihamoni. The head of government is a member of the majority party or coalition, named prime minister by the Chairman of the National Assembly, and appointed by the king; the prime minister in 2008 was Hun Sen. The Council of Ministers, or cabinet, is appointed by the monarch on the advice of the prime minister.

The legislature is bicameral, consisting of the National Assembly of 123 members elected by popular vote to serve five-year terms, and the Senate of sixty-one members, two appointed by the King, two elected by the National  Assembly, and fifty-seven elected to serve five-year terms by parliamentarians and commune councils. The judiciary consists of the Supreme Council of the Magistracy overseeing the Supreme Court and lower courts. The legal system is a mixture of French-influenced codes from the United Nations Transitional Authority in Cambodia (UNTAC) period, royal decrees, and Acts of the legislature, with influences from customary law and remnants of Communist legal theory.

The country is divided into twenty provinces and four municipalities with their own local governments. The actual balance of power between the political parties and their interests and those of the central and provincial governments provides room for parties and their leaders to maneuver for advantage.

VALUES &
ATTITUDES

RELIGION AND VALUES

The great religions of Hinduism and Buddhism
have permeated Asian
culture over centuries,
giving rise to a set of core
values shared by all Asian
countries, including
Cambodia. Underlying
both religions are earlier
animistic beliefs that are
commonly held
throughout the region.
The core Asian values
embrace faith, respect,
hierarchy, nonconfrontation, consensus, group
identity, self-control, and politeness and manners.

Faith

While members of Asian societies may belong to
one of a number of religious faiths, many do not.
In modern times ideology has often taken the
place of religious faith and has served much the
same function by focusing loyalty upon a leader
and a set of beliefs, inculcating belief in his

message, and demanding public demonstration of that belief. In the last half century Communism has attempted to play such a role. In Southeast Asian society the codes and beliefs that govern, or at least influence, behavior are underpinned by Hinduism and Buddhism, influencing even people who would not claim to be either.

Respect

Traditional Asian countries believe in a society in which respect is given to others according to their place in that society.

Hierarchy

Society is regarded as hierarchical, and those lower in the hierarchy show respect to those above them. Hierarchies may exist within the political system, the family, the social system, the business community, and in other walks of life. These

hierarchies are not necessarily based on political, social, or economic power. Ideally, those higher in the hierarchy also respect the place and role of those below them.

Consensus
To maintain harmony, decisions should be arrived at by discussion and mutual consent—often a time-consuming process.

Group Identity
"No man is an island." All persons have a position in society that gives them an identity within a group.

Self-Control
A person should remain calm and retain control of his or her emotions and behavior. Foreigners who shout or swear, make threatening or derogatory gestures, or go off in a huff and slam the door may express their feelings, but they lose the respect of any Cambodians who might be present. Excessive demonstrations of affection and friendship, especially in public, are also embarrassing for Cambodians to witness or receive.

Politeness and Manners
Politeness is the expression of respect between members of society, and manners are the means and outward signs by which that politeness is expressed. Politeness and manners are the

lubricants of social discourse. Their forms of expression signify the hierarchy and status of individuals within society.

"Victorian" Values
Cambodian social values are not so different from Western values as they were a few generations ago. Think back in time. What did your grandparents or great-grandparents regard as polite behavior in the home and in society? Emulate them, and you won't go far wrong in Cambodia.

Some commentators in the West have argued that Asian values facilitate the creation of authoritarian states wherein the people defer to those who govern them in the name of the collective, conformist, consensual society. Others see in them a means of maintaining social order and harmony. As a visitor, you will win respect by attempting to conform to them, and lose it by disregarding them—although their own good manners may prevent your Asian companions from openly commenting or reacting.

In business meetings and negotiations, and in public, where your status and character are being assessed, the visitor should always conform to standards of behavior that will earn respect.

Among the younger generation of Cambodians, especially those who have studied, worked, or traveled overseas and those exposed to Western culture through films and television, attitudes and behavior are changing, particularly in interaction with each other. In such cases you may find a friendly and familiar rapport, and be able to act as you would in your own environment. This is most likely to occur in Phnom Penh, the large towns, and the tourist areas. However, always, at a first meeting, and in case of doubt, behave with some formality.

THE FAMILY

The family lies at the core of Cambodian society and is the main expression of group identity. Here, "family" means the extended family. Traditionally—and this is still the case in the countryside in particular—the family provides security, labor, social security, a place in broader society, status, occupation, and identity. Social life revolves around the family, and respect is accorded to senior members. The family places responsibility upon all its members, but also provides support to all, and family celebrations are of great importance, reinforcing family bonds.

The family was a target of the Khmer Rouge, and suffered severe disruption as family members were turned against each other by indoctrination or fear. Those years hang as a shadow over many families, but the institution, and trust in its values, is being renewed as time passes. A new threat to the traditional family may be the inroads of Western values as the economy diversifies, outside media become increasingly accessible, and more young people receive a higher education and travel more widely. Nevertheless, visit a Cambodian house and you may be surprised at the number of people you find there who are part of the extended family.

Family among the Khmer is less rigidly defined than among the Chinese and Vietnamese, whose cultures have an element of ancestor worship. Khmers of noble descent may trace their lineage over several generations, but for the majority of Khmers the family is a looser structure, encompassing the nuclear family of husband, wife, and children, and extending to grandparents, uncles, aunts, nieces, nephews, and first cousins, many of whom may live in the same household or nearby, particularly in the rural areas. However, there is no tradition of family names among ordinary Khmers, and genealogies rarely extend back more that three generations. Khmer relationships are therefore set more in place than time, with people having strong attachment to their community, village, and province.

A Cause for Concern

It is difficult for most Cambodians to understand the idea of the purely nuclear family, or of a situation where a couple may not wish to have children. Speaking to a Cambodian lady, an acquaintance mentioned that she and her husband, married for some years, had no children. The Cambodian woman's response was to reach out her hand and say, "I am so sorry."

Older family members are treated with respect, and addressed with terms denoting their status. Thus an older man will be addressed as *Ta* (grandfather), *Po* (uncle), or *Bang* (brother); and an older woman will be addressed as *Yeay* (grandmother), *Ming* (aunt), or *Bang Srei* (sister). These terms are also used respectfully by younger people in addressing older people who are not related to them.

In recent years changes have been taking place in family relationships, particularly in urban areas. The clear demarcation between male and female roles, still evident in rural areas, has broken down to varying extents among the urban population. The role of the husband is being challenged by a new generation of educated women. The traditional arranged marriage is under threat from romantic notions from the West. Nevertheless, the traditional responsibilities and obligations between the generations still underpin Cambodian society and the extended family, the young paying respect to their elders and providing care in their old age, and the elders extending care, protection, and love to the young. These roles remain important, as your visits to families in their homes will testify.

ATTITUDES TO TIME

Cambodians traditionally have a casual attitude to time, and in personal life particularly time is flexible. The casual approach is less marked in towns and cities, where business hours for government offices and companies provide a structure for the day. However, individuals may not necessarily be punctual in meeting those times. In the world of religion, within the temples (*pagodas*) and monasteries (*wats*) set times for worship and prayer also provide structure. In the business world, on the whole, those with whom you have professional and business dealings will be punctual. Government offices are less rigorous, and there is still the attitude that matters should take their course and time should be stretched to accommodate them.

A factor to bear in mind is that respect is based on age and seniority. It is important not to keep an elder or superior waiting, because that would show disrespect. It would also show disrespect to bring a meeting with a superior to a hasty end—unless you are on your way to meet someone else of higher rank. When setting up meetings, allow plenty of time to go through the proposed business without haste, and indicate whether you are meeting anyone of higher seniority later.

ATTITUDES TO FOREIGNERS

Cambodians are generally welcoming, polite, and easygoing, and will make allowances for the behavior of foreigners. With the growth of the tourist industry and access to international media there is a greater awareness of outside people and cultures. Nevertheless, they will appreciate any efforts you may make to use their language and respect their codes of behavior and etiquette. Despite the trauma of recent years they are proud of their ancient culture and anxious to retain their sense of identity as they modernize and Westernize. They will respond to evidence that you respect their culture and traditions.

Visitors should remember that the events that took place under the Khmer Rouge regime are not openly discussed. Those who survived the regime are burdened with their memories, and try to forget; younger people know only what they may have been told by their families. The generation still in power has retained certain tangible reminders, such as the Genocide Museum at Tuol Seng, where confessions were extracted under torture, and the "Killing Fields" at Choeung Ek.

ATTITUDES TO ASIAN NEIGHBORS

Cambodians' attitudes to their Asian neighbors are complex. Over their long history, kept alive by the importance of Angkor and its monuments and art, the Khmers' relations with their neighbors have included both triumph and humiliation. We have seen in recent history how porous those borders are to incursions and how recently territories that now constitute the nation of Cambodia were in others' hands. Their relations with the Thais and Vietnamese have been the most complex, as we have seen in the history section of Chapter 1. Official relations with all within ASEAN, which is dedicated to mutual growth and development, are now good.

ATTITUDES TO MINORITIES

These political events have impinged to some extent on the attitudes of ordinary Khmers, who retain some wariness toward Thai, Vietnamese, and Chinese people within Cambodia. The Chinese suffered persecution under both the Lon Nol and Khmer Rouge regimes. Lon Nol and his offices resented Chinese dominance in commerce and acted against the Chinese commercial class to further their own commercial and business interests. The Khmer Rouge persecuted all who were not rural peasants, and all Chinese, living as they do in the cities and towns, suffered. At the present time the Chinese who are Cambodian citizens are benefiting from the economic improvements and the government's improved relations with China.

Relations between Khmers and the Cambodian Vietnamese are better now that conflict on their border has ended, but the Vietnamese are generally looked down upon by the Khmer majority and are among the most disadvantaged. Relations with those few communities of Chams that still live in Cambodia appear to be good. Although the Chams practice Islam and retain their own sense of identity, the two communities coexist peacefully.

The Chunchiet or Khmer Loeu, who live in the mountainous northeast border regions, are generally little known by ordinary Cambodians, and are occasionally persecuted by their immediate neighbors. The have become the victims of exploitation of Cambodia's forest and mineral resources, but are largely ignored.

With the opening of Cambodia again to the world, visitors from a wide range of cultures have come to the country, mostly as tourists. During the UNTAC period the United Nations personnel were from varied backgrounds and Cambodians are also now accustomed to seeing people of all nationalities and races on television. Africans and black citizens of other nations visiting Cambodia will attract attention, but so do all non-Asian visitors. In general all will be welcomed as guests and treated as such with the courtesy, friendly interest, and hospitality natural to most Cambodians.

RELIGION &
FESTIVALS

RELIGIONS OF CAMBODIA

Cambodia has a rich religious tradition. Most Cambodians today practice Theravada Buddhism (sometimes referred as Hinayana Buddhism), but some practices and traditions are based on Hinduism. As we have seen, both religions flourished during the early centuries CE, although Hinduism captured the allegiance of the early rulers of Angkor. The most revered Hindu deities were Shiva and Vishnu, for a time embodied together in the form of a single deity known as Marinara. The kings of the early Angkor period favored Shiva, superseded by Vishnu in the twelfth century. In the thirteenth and fourteenth centuries, Theravada Buddhism became firmly established, having entered Cambodia from India through Southeast Asia. The changes in religious allegiance are clearly demarcated in the temples and shrines at Angkor. Despite the triumph of Buddhism, however, elements of Hinduism survived and are still present in the rituals and customs associated with those fundamental rites of passage of birth, marriage, and death.

Theravada Buddhism teaches the concept of *nirvana*, or total extinction of all desire and suffering to arrive at the final level of reincarnation. This state may be hastened by the performance of good works, by meditation and contemplation, and by making donations to temples and shrines to support the monks who have dedicated themselves to a life of poverty and prayer. Traditionally, all young men were expected to become monks between leaving school and taking up a career or attaining marriage—a kind of spiritual "gap year." The tradition survives, but the time spent as a monk has for most been reduced to a token fifteen days, or even less. Nevertheless, Buddhism remains a potent force in society, having survived the widespread destruction and killings of the Khmer Rouge to be reinstated as the state religion.

Islam is the religion of the descendants of the Chams, who migrated from Vietnam after the defeat of Champa by the Vietnamese in 1472. The call to prayer is by beating a drum, as is done by the Buddhists. The Khmer Rouge conducted a concerted campaign against the Muslims, but the community is staging a revival.

Christianity was introduced with limited success by the French and made some headway in the cities, particularly Phnom Penh. Christians also suffered under the Khmer Rouge, and have made a comeback, but remain a small minority.

Animism

Prior to the introduction of Hinduism and Buddhism, Cambodians were animists, and animist beliefs persist, particularly with regard to fertility, the soil, and the people's link to the land. Animists worship the spirits of the land and sky and of their ancestors. Animism has been subsumed into the other major faiths, but is still practiced in its purest form by the Khmer Loeu, or hill tribes. However, many Cambodians believe that spirits of the departed still inhabit their familiar surroundings even after death, awaiting their transition to the next life. Spirit houses are erected to placate these spirits, especially if their familiar surroundings have been altered. When a new house is built or a new building is erected a spirit house is provided to house the disinherited spirits, usually at a little distance from the new building. Cambodians will offer gifts of flowers, incense, food, and drink to the spirits, to placate them and to seek their blessing.

Beliefs in evil and malicious spirits also persist. Such spirits bring misfortune and sickness. Certain plants are thought to deter them, as is having a raised doorstep or a carved figure to ward them off.

Making offerings to the good spirits inhabiting the spirit house is also seen as acquiring their assistance to ward off the evil spirits or to resist evil.

FESTIVALS AND NATIONAL CELEBRATIONS

Festivals are celebrated according to the lunar calendar, and thus the dates according to the Gregorian calendar change from year to year. They are in most cases also public holidays. Diaries published in Cambodia give the dates for each lunar festival, and also the dates of the public holidays linked to them.

Chaul Chnam Chen (Lunar New Year)

Ethnic Chinese and Vietnamese celebrate this festival in late January or early February. The festival lasts over fifteen days, with the first and last days being the most publicly celebrated.

Chinese and Vietnamese shops close for at least part of the time, and visits are made between family and friends. If invited to the house of a friend or colleague, take a small gift of money for the children (in Chinese an *ang pau*). *Ang pau* envelopes are available at Chinese stores, and the gift should consist of new notes. Dress should be smart and conservative on such occasions. In most cases men will not be required to wear a tie, but seek advice from Chinese and Vietnamese friends and colleagues or from expatriates with some experience as to what is expected in terms of attire. It is possible that you will be attending the open house of a person of rank, and men may be required to wear a suit. If you are visiting Chinese and Vietnamese friends, or the home of an employee or servant, "smart casual" would apply.

Chaul Chnam (Khmer New Year)

This is celebrated for three days in mid-April, bringing the country to a standstill. It is a noisy and tumultuous event as social restraints are loosened, and water and talcum powder, often colored, are thrown at and over all and sundry.

Chat Preah Nenkal (Royal Plowing Festival)

This takes place in early May in front of the National Museum near the Royal Palace in Phnom Penh. Two Royal Oxen plow a furrow to symbolize the king's role as a source of fertility and plenty.

Visaka Puja

Falling on the eighth day of the fourth moon in May or June, Visaka Puja celebrates Buddha's birth, enlightenment, and passing away. Candlelit processions of monks take place at *wats* and pagodas, with the most evocative at Angkor Wat.

P'chun Ben

Falling between mid-September and early October, this event also centers on the *wats*. Offerings of food and drink are made by individuals and families to the dead through the monks, and paper money is burned.

Bon Om Tuk

In early November, Bon Om Tuk celebrates the naval victory of Jayavarman VII over the Chams in 1181, and also marks the end of the wet season and the reversal of the current of the Tonle Sap River, as water that has raised the level of the Tonle Sap Lake during the wet season begins to drain out

into the Mekong. It is, therefore, perhaps the most significant festival for the country, and is celebrated with great excitement, with boat races on the Tonle Sap and Mekong Rivers.

PUBLIC HOLIDAYS

These are state holidays, dated according to the Gregorian calendar, and include internationally recognized observances and anniversaries of events relating to the Cambodian state and its history. Including those public holidays associated with the festivals mentioned above, Cambodians enjoy more public holidays than most people. If the dates for holidays fall on a weekend, the holidays are taken during the following week. Cambodians will also take an extra day or two off work during the major festivals and celebrations.

January 1	International New Year's Day
January 7	Victory over the Genocide
March 8	International Women's Day
April 13	Khmer New Year
May 1	International Labor Day
May 1	International Children's Day
May 13-15	King Sihamoni's Birthday
September 24	Constitution Day
October 23	Paris Peace Accords
October 31	King Father's Birthday
November 9	Independence Day
December 10	International Human Rights Day

RITES OF PASSAGE

Birth, marriage, and death are universally recognized rites of passage, and are as important in Cambodia as elsewhere. Non-Buddhists follow the ritual of their faith, but many of the practices surrounding birth, marriage, and death are cultural rather than specific to Buddhism.

Birth

As in all cultures, the birth of a child is a significant and welcome event. Traditionally a woman was assisted by a birth attendant or midwife, usually an older woman who had learned from experience attending births within the family or within her community. This practice persists in rural communities, but these days such women will in most cases have received some training in hygiene and basic awareness of possible complications that may require referral to a clinic or hospital. In urban areas women have access to a hospital or clinic providing medical attention.

Traditionally, Cambodians believed that the woman's body must be warmed after the birth, as must the baby, often referred to as "roasting." After the birth, the baby was wrapped in cloth and the woman covered. A common practice was for the mother and baby to lie on a bed above or close to a fire for up to a week. During this time the woman might be sponged with warm water, but may not wash or shower in cold water. Other practices included the woman sitting on a fire-warmed stone, or lying with such a stone on her abdomen; and steaming, whereby the woman was encouraged to sweat out impurities over steam from boiling water with a mixture of herbs, during or after which she might apply a pounded mixture of galangal and turmeric root to her body. These practices were said to make the uterus shrink, prevent sagging of the stomach, and combat illness. Over the same period the woman was encouraged to eat spicy food, such as pork or fish prepared and cooked with black pepper and ginger, and to drink large quantities of a concoction of herbs boiled in water with rice wine.

Whatever the medicinal virtues of this traditional regime, it also served the purpose of ensuring the woman had a period of rest and attention after the birth and time to devote to the baby, before returning to the realities of what for many is still a hard existence. Today these traditional practices are less observed, or have been adapted depending on access to modern medical procedures. However, many medical personnel died under the Khmer Rouge regime and training was interrupted, so there is a shortage of trained midwives—a situation that the government is trying to remedy. Meanwhile, although traditional midwives have received basic training in modern midwifery practice, the old ideas, like "roasting," die hard.

Marriage

Marriages are still arranged in Cambodia, usually by the families concerned. Astrologers may be called in to compute whether the proposed partners are compatible, and use is made of a go-between to negotiate the dowry. Often partners are found from different branches of large extended families, but marriage between close blood relatives is forbidden. Parents often look out for suitable partners for their children and make contact through a go-between with the other family so that an understanding may be arrived at while the proposed partners are young. The traditional deference of youth to age caused young people to accept such arrangements in the past, taking the situation for granted. Among the educated young, exposed increasingly to the romantic ideas of the West, the system is being challenged as they meet and work with other young people of similar background and outside their parents' circle of family, friends, and acquaintances. These situations often lead to family distress, but the arranged marriage is becoming less common, especially in the cities and towns. In the rural areas, the old traditions persist partly because the range of choice of marriage partners is restricted.

The traditional Khmer wedding ceremony symbolically re-creates the marriage of Preah Thong, the first Khmer ruler, to the *Naga* princess

Neang Neak. According to legend, Preah Thong was wandering in exile from his homeland when he met and fell in love with Neang Neak. Her father sanctioned the marriage and, as a gift to the happy couple, swallowed a part of the ocean and thus created the land of Cambodia. A Khmer wedding, therefore, has all the splendor and ceremony of a royal wedding, with the groom and his bride, dressed as royalty, being prince and princess for the day. Family, friends, and other members of the community join in, and musicians perform on traditional instruments. Once spread over three days, the ceremonies now usually take place on one day.

In the morning the groom and his family and friends go in noisy procession to the home of the bride, bearing wrapped platters of fruit and Khmer desserts. They are accompanied by musicians and singers and are met by a representative of the bride's family, who inspects the gifts and, if of sufficient quality and quantity, begins a humorous verbal exchange with the representative of the groom, which ends with the groom and his followers being invited into the bride's home.

The bride and groom are seated for the ceremony, in which the spirits of the ancestors of the two families are invoked, and all those present are invited to observe and bless the wedding. The couple are then blessed by three, five, or sometimes seven monks, before undergoing an elaborate cleansing ceremony during which the parents of the bride and groom and their relatives and friends take turns to symbolically cut the hair of the couple and wish them well. Following the hair-cutting ceremony, married couples form a circle around the bride and groom; three candles are lit and passed around the circle clockwise seven times, each person passing his or her hand over the flame in a sweeping motion toward the couple as a silent blessing. Only married couples may participate, because it is believed that they will pass on to the bride and groom the secret quality that has preserved their own union.

The wedding ends with the knot-tying ceremony, in which the guests come forward with their blessing to the new couple and tie ribbons around the wrists of each. Traditionally these were to be worn for three days for good luck. At this stage photos may be taken of each guest with the couple.

Except for the blessing by the monks, which is done in silence, songs appropriate to each stage of the ceremony accompany the ritual, and music is played on traditional instruments.

Celebrations end with feasting, drinking, and dancing. In the cities and among the wealthier members of society, the postnuptial celebration is held in a restaurant. In the rural areas, and in the case of poorer families, the families get together to organize the celebration, erecting awnings and preparing food.

Should you be invited to a wedding, seek advice from your Cambodian colleagues and friends as to what to expect. Customs are changing, especially in the cities, although the traditional pattern remains. As a gift to the couple, discreetly present money in new notes in an envelope, either to the couple as you leave or to a person acting on their behalf. Again, consult with your colleagues or friends as to the accepted practice and whom to approach.

Death

While grief is felt and expressed at death, it is tempered among the Buddhist Khmer by the belief that it is not only the end of this life but the beginning of another, better life. After death, the body is washed, dressed, and placed in a coffin, which is usually decorated with flowers and displays a photograph of the deceased. White pennants, known as white crocodile flags, are hung outside the house to signify that a death has taken place. Chanting and mourning music, nowadays often amplified, is played during the mourning period, which may be for one or two days, during which mourners are received and fed. Buddhist Khmer are usually cremated and the body is taken in procession to the temple for cremation. The procession is accompanied by an *achar*, or master of ceremony, and is made up of Buddhist monks, members of the family, and other mourners. The immediate family shave their heads and dress in white, and music is provided by hired musicians. After the cremation relics of the dead such as teeth and fragments of bone are often collected to be worn on gold chains as amulets.

MAKING
FRIENDS

SOCIAL BEHAVIOR

Behavior in Cambodian society is governed by the
factors discussed in the previous chapter: showing
respect, observing the social hierarchy by
deferring to age and position attained, behaving
and dressing modestly, and maintaining harmony
by avoiding confrontation by politeness and good
manners. In all social situations it is advisable to
find out, whenever possible, the age, status, and
relationship of those present. In most cases, as
you are introduced to people, you will be told
who they are and their status or position,
according to the context in which you are meeting
them. In fact, this is fairly similar to what is done
in any Western social situation.

GREETINGS

Although the pace of modernization and
Westernization is quickening, Cambodians as a
people still observe certain social practices
common throughout Southeast Asia. The
traditional greeting is the *som pas*, in which the

palms are held together as in prayer, and lifted to chest level with a slight bow. On meeting, Cambodians will perform the *som pas* and say, "*Chum reeup sooa.*" On departing they will again perform the *som pas,* and say, "*Chum reeup lear.*"

In the cities and tourist areas where Western influences are more marked, the handshake has become common between men, but women are more reluctant, out of modesty, to shake hands, particularly with men.

It is important to demonstrate respect for elder members of the family or for those with status in society, including monks. When meeting, if in the open and you are wearing a hat, it is polite to remove the hat and bow your head. The head is regarded as the center of intelligence and of spirituality. As such it is sacred. By bowing the head a person shows respect.

DRESS

If you are visiting Cambodia briefly in an official or business capacity, your first meetings will probably be in somewhat formal surroundings, and your dress should match them—smart, formal, and conservative. Urban, professional Cambodians generally wear Western-style clothing at work.

If you are working longer-term in the country, you will probably find that dress in the workplace is much as you are used to. Offices are air-conditioned, and the men may wear jackets. If in doubt, dress conservatively, wearing a jacket and tie if you are a man, and similarly smart and modest clothing if you are a woman. You can always dress "down" if you find that this is the normal practice where you are working. When taking up employment or visiting in a business or professional capacity, you could ask your contacts the accepted dress code.

Observing and respecting the accepted codes of dress and behavior will win you the respect of the people among whom you work and live. In the tourist areas, Cambodians will tolerate standards of dress and behavior from tourists that they would otherwise regard with some disdain. Also, in the bigger towns and cities and among the young, Western dress is common and behavior less restrained. Nevertheless, as a visitor, you should respect local codes and dress and behave accordingly.

Thus women should dress modestly, and men should have on a shirt and trousers for going around town, rather than wearing shorts or going bare-chested. The latter is all right on the beach, but not on the streets, and is definitely unacceptable in the *wats* and pagodas.

INVITATIONS

If you are resident in the country for any length of time, you will meet Cambodians who will invite you home for a meal. In a family context you will be introduced to the older members of the family first, and if they are older than you, you should be the first to perform the *som pas*. If there are family members younger than you they will greet you after their elders and perform the *som pas,* to which you may respond with the same gesture or a bow of the head. If friendship develops and you are a guest more often, then the same pattern will apply but the gestures may be less formal.

More commonly, you will be invited to meet in a restaurant. At other times you may meet informally, or perhaps accidentally, in a public place. The following points of etiquette should help you avoid embarrassment whatever the circumstances.

DOS AND DON'TS

- When visiting someone at home a small
gift expressing your gratitude is not
obligatory, but would be appreciated.
Value is less important than appearance, so
some attractive little object, perhaps from
your home country, would be appropriate,
neatly and colorfully wrapped. Don't use
white paper, because white is associated
with death and mourning.

- Cambodians remove their shoes when
entering a house. They will do so when
entering yours, too, even if you tell them
not to bother. Removing shoes is a sign of
respect. This is also the case when entering
a temple. The same may apply when
entering a guesthouse or some restaurants.
In such cases there will generally be a pile of
shoes at or near the entrance.

- Be sure to note carefully where you leave
your shoes when you are visiting a temple or
any other place where a number of people
are visiting. It can be frustrating to search
for a pair of shoes you cannot immediately
locate—and perhaps even more frustrating
to find one and not the other!

- Remove your hat. Cambodians wear hats
for protection from the sun and rain, and

regard them as items for outdoor wear only. To wear one inside is disrespectful. Again, one sees the similarity with Western formal dress code and practice.

- A guest is always offered a drink of water, tea, or fruit juice. Sometimes food may be offered. It is polite to accept, even if you only take a sip or a bite.

- In some houses you may be offered a chair, but in others there may be mats to sit on. If that is the case, sit with your legs folded together, with feet back, to one side. Don't sit with your feet straight out, with the soles facing those in front of you, and don't sit with your legs either apart or crossed.

- Never touch or pat an adult or older child on the head, for this would be regarded as an insult. In the unlikely event of its being necessary to touch a person's head—if removing something entangled in the hair or treating a wound, for instance—ask permission, and explain why. Here again, Western etiquette is not dissimilar—one would normally explain and excuse oneself before performing such an action.

- To summon someone, never beckon with an upraised finger or upraised palm, which have suggestive connotations. Motion with your right hand held palm down.

- When passing things to other people, use both hands, or the right hand only, never the left, which is considered unclean.

- If your meeting is within a business context, have business cards ready to hand out to all present, using both hands and making a slight bow.

- Never use your left hand for eating.

- When eating with chopsticks never leave the chopsticks in the bowl with ends pointing upward. They resemble the incense sticks burned for the dead. Instead, place them at the side of your plate or bowl.

- Toothpicks are usually provided at table. When using one, it is polite to cover your mouth with the other hand.

- Nevertheless, social attitudes are changing and younger Cambodians and those who have been overseas for education and training will have picked up Western ways and will want to demonstrate their new sophistication. In their company the social strictures may be more relaxed, but err on the conservative side until any relationship has been established on a more casual mode. Even then, you will realize that the traditional codes regarding gesture persist and as a visitor to the country it is only polite to respect them.

- Should you stay in the country, possibly to work, and you establish a close friendship, you may become regarded as one of the family, Should this happen, you may find yourself regarded as an honorary "uncle" or "aunt" and accepting certain obligations. In particular you may feel obliged to take on some supportive role, particularly for a younger member of the family, perhaps in assisting in education or access to employment.

THE CAMBODIANS AT HOME

HOUSING

Housing varies enormously, from the palaces of the royal family to the most humble wooden rural dwellings. High-ranking members of the government and the bureaucracy now occupy the gracious houses of their onetime colonial masters,

as do many of the rich and successful in business and commerce. In the newer suburban areas are spacious houses and apartments for the well-off middle and professional classes. Such houses and apartments will have four bedrooms, possibly three bathrooms, a sitting and dining area, a kitchen, a utility room, and, particularly in a house, quarters for one or more servants. There will be space for parking one or two cars. Some will be walled and gated, with a watchman.

In the cities and larger towns are high-rise apartment blocks. Those designed for and rented by the urban working class may suffer from neglect and appear shabby, as tenements often do, and the streets of poorer areas of cities and towns may be untidy and unpleasant to walk through.

A feature of central urban areas is the rows of usually Chinese-owned or rented shop-houses, to be found also in suburban and town centers. The shops, closed by shutters at night, open on to the street. They may be piled with goods, or furnished with cabinets, shelves, and counters, depending on the goods sold. The shop owners and their families—often their extended families—live upstairs in what may be quite spacious living accommodation.

In rural areas one sees similar shop-houses, which may be built of wood rather than concrete, again housing an extended family. On the waterways are moored houseboats and wooden

stilted houses rising from the water and mud, and even floating villages, as on the Tonle Sap Lake.

A feature common to all types of houses, including those of the very poor, is their cleanliness. Outside the house may be cluttered, for the poor do not readily throw items away or live in areas where the garbage is regularly collected; but inside houses and apartments are clean and well swept. The well-off have servants to clean for them, but cleanliness, both personal and in the home, is a feature in Southeast Asian culture, and even the poorest of houses is neatly swept. Such customs as the removal of footwear aid in this.

Since the return of peace to Cambodia there has been rising prosperity and the creation of an urban society similar to that found in its prosperous neighbors. As a visitor living and working in the country you will probably enter a number of homes when visiting colleagues and friends, both expatriate and Cambodian, both well-off and not so well-off. As an expatriate you will enjoy good housing with modern amenities and a comfortable standard of living. One common factor is the hospitality you will receive from your colleagues and from the growing circles of friends and acquaintances you will establish.

DAILY LIFE AND ROUTINE

Cambodians generally rise early to enjoy the cool of the morning, and often rest during the heat of the early afternoon. When work finishes in the late afternoon they make full use of the cool evenings and walk out to visit friends or eat at local restaurants and stalls.

The Working Day

Government offices are open from 7:30 to 11:30 a.m., when they close for siesta, then open again from 2:30 p.m. until 5:00 p.m. However, there will generally be few people in their offices early, and few after 4:00 p.m. Business hours for larger firms are 8:00 a.m. to 12 noon and 2:00 to 5:30 p.m. Banking hours may vary slightly according to the individual bank, but most are open from 8:30 a.m. to 3:30 p.m. on weekdays and on Saturday mornings.

Museums and tourist attractions are generally open seven days a week including the lunch hour.

Local restaurants are generally open from 6:30 a.m. to 9:00 p.m. International restaurants stay open a little later. Bars that serve food are open all day; others open only in the evenings. Nightclubs are to be found in Phnom Penh, Siem Reap, and the larger towns and tourist areas.

Local markets are open seven days a week, from 6:30 a.m. to 5:30 p.m.

Your local friends and colleagues will soon point out the best places to eat, drink, and shop.

Shopping

In recent years the range of shops and goods available has greatly improved, especially in Phnom Penh and Siem Reap, but in other urban areas as well. In the shopping centers you will find everything you need, whether as a long-term visitor employed in the country and setting up home or as a tourist passing through. Supermarkets can provide all your food and domestic requirements, including imported products that will be familiar to you. The smaller family-run general stores carry a wide range of goods, and there are specialist outlets for electrical and photographic equipment, clothing, furniture, and personal and household needs. Multistory shopping centers are the modern equivalent of the traditional bazaars and markets, and house individual shops and cafés, but also include department stores and supermarkets.

In the older shopping areas, with their traditional shop-houses, a similar supply of goods and services can be found. Bakeries, producing a range of breads and cakes, are a legacy of French colonialism. Finally there are markets, both open and covered,

which carry a wide range of goods and produce. Bear in mind that Cambodia's textile industry has expanded greatly, and designer products can slip into the local markets and be obtained cheaply. Be warned that designer labels sometimes appear on inferior products. In fact, you may even see the labels alone on sale!

The shopping areas and markets all have restaurants, cafés, and food and drink stalls offering a range of cuisines of varying sophistication. A shopping expedition can be full of variety and interest, and stopping for a drink or snack at a stall or café offers a great opportunity for people-watching!

Bargaining

Be prepared for some gentle bargaining in the tourist areas and local markets. The Khmer are not aggressive bargainers, but it is acceptable to try to settle on a lower price than that first suggested. Merely showing a disinclination to buy will encourage a lower offer from the vendor. However, in the general household goods and grocery shop-houses, where you may do your ordinary shopping, bear in mind that you, as a visitor, are infinitely better off than those who are selling to you, and that a small premium will not greatly affect you. You may find that, if you frequent particular shops or market stalls, you will get a better price once shopkeepers and vendors recognize you as a regular customer.

THE FAMILY

The nuclear family, of husband, wife, and unmarried children, is the main unit within the family structure. Emotional ties are strong, and are reinforced by mutual support such as aid in time of trouble; economic cooperation in the sharing of labor, produce, and income; and the sharing of religious and ceremonial obligations and duties. In the cities, the broader family, embracing grandparents, uncles, aunts, cousins, nieces, and nephews, may also form part of the household. In rural areas, the extended family, often living together or within easy reach, is an important element of village life. Families work together as a unit to help each other and their neighbors in labor-intensive tasks such as house building and other work associated with maintaining the village infrastructure—buildings, paths, drains, and irrigation, for example. In the towns and cities, as in the villages, the family participates in the religious life of the temple. These shared responsibilities, obligations, and services provide cohesion within both the family and the broader community.

Within the family the husband is legally head,

but the wife has considerable authority in her domestic role as controller of the family budget. She also takes on the principal ethical and religious role in bringing up the children. In rural areas there is an obvious division of labor, with the men performing the harder physical labor, such as plowing and harrowing the rice fields, caring for the cattle, buying and selling livestock, and repairing and maintaining the structure of the house. Women are mainly involved in planting, reaping, and winnowing the rice crop, tending gardens, weaving, and handling the household money. Men and women work together in the rice fields as the need arises.

Children

Children are shown affection and considerable freedom until about the age of four, when they are expected to be able to bathe and feed themselves, then from the age of five or six they may be expected to look after their younger siblings. By the time they enter school at around seven, children

have learned to respect their elders and to play a role in family life, the girls helping the mother with her tasks and the boys working with their fathers in the fields and with the livestock in the country or in their business or with other activities in the urban areas. Class differences are a factor, with the children of the better-off having a more privileged existence and more contact with servants. Nevertheless, the overall experience of children's upbringing emphasizes socialization, obedience, and respect for one's elders, including Buddhist monks. Even traditional children's games emphasize co-operation, skill, and social participation rather than winning or losing.

If you are visiting Cambodia with your family, you will find everything you need for babies and children in Phnom Penh and Siem Reap, and increasingly also in the other large towns. You will find that your children become centers of attention! Take the opportunity to explain to them the social attitudes of their new Cambodian companions. If your children learn to demonstrate respect to the elders and monks they may meet, their own experience will be all the more positive and enjoyable.

EDUCATION

Education in Cambodia was severely disrupted by the Khmer Rouge. Educated and qualified people, including teachers and monks, were targeted and killed or sent to labor camps where many died. Education in any meaningful sense ceased. By the end of the Khmer Rouge period, over 75 percent of all educators had died or had fled the country. Beginning in 1979, the PRK government, hampered by continuing civil strife, began to revive the education system, but, although the system now embraces the range from preschool to university, it is hampered by poorly educated, poorly trained, and poorly paid teachers, large class sizes, and outdated teaching methods, with great variation across the country.

The constitution prescribes nine years' free compulsory education, but its provision is administered at three levels—central, provincial, and district—and corruption, poverty, and family dependence upon child labor, especially in the rural areas, has resulted in uneven provision and attendance. At higher levels, the shortage of qualified teachers and of adequate places in secondary classes has led to corruption, with parents paying bribes to examiners and to obtain university places. Nevertheless progress is being made toward improving the provision and standard of government education. For those who can afford it, of course, there is

access to private education and to institutions overseas. One notable feature of Cambodian towns is the emergence from the most humble dwellings of well-scrubbed and neatly dressed children on their way to school in the mornings.

If moving to Cambodia with your family, seek advice from your employers and expatriate contacts on education. Many expatriates send older children to boarding school in their home countries, but there are several international schools in Phnom Penh. The International School of Phnom Penh takes children through to year twelve, and offers the International Baccalaureate. The Northbridge International School Cambodia operates a US-style curriculum from preschool to year twelve. The British International School operates a British curriculum and has a Montessori junior school. There is also a British International School at Siem Reap.

ENTERTAINING

Cambodians rarely entertain formally at home, though this is changing among the new middle and professional classes. If you are invited to dinner at someone's home, you will find it both a formal and a family affair. Elders to children will be present, and you will be an honored guest. Your host will probably be able to converse in English, but others present may not. If the host is not fluent in English himself he may also invite someone who can translate.

Cambodian table manners are fairly formal. If you are unsure of local etiquette, observe what others do. Many Cambodians still eat seated on the floor, sitting in the lotus position or with legs to one side; sometimes they sit on low benches or chairs. As a visitor, you may be offered a chair. The urban middle classes commonly use tables and chairs, especially for entertaining. The traditional welcoming drink is a cup of hot tea, after which food is served. The food may arrive in communal dishes, from which each diner helps himself on to his own plate or bowl. The courses will usually be meat, fish, and vegetables in a variety of styles and served in no particular order. Your host or the person seated next to you may offer you special delicacies. During the meal there will be tea or water to drink. Eating utensils will be either chopsticks or a spoon and fork, the fork held in the left hand and the spoon in the right. Food is eaten from the spoon, the fork being used only to push it on to the spoon. As the left hand is unclean, it is important not to let it touch the food.

TABLE MANNERS

- Wait to be told where to sit. The most senior person is usually seated first.
- Don't start eating until the most senior person has started.
- If the host chooses some food and puts it on your plate, you should eat it.
- Leave something in your bowl or on your plate to indicate that your appetite has been satisfied.
- When eating with chopsticks, never leave them in the bowl with the ends pointing upward. They resemble the incense sticks that are burned for the dead. Instead, place them at the side of your plate or bowl.

An expatriate working with Cambodians may be invited to a restaurant, perhaps along with other expatriate and Cambodian colleagues and friends of the host. In such cases, the meal will proceed much as described above. At these occasions, alcohol, mainly beer, may be served, especially if there are no women present. A business function may also bring people together as a group to eat and drink, but a stand-up reception or cocktail party is not usual.

Entertaining Cambodians

If you yourself are the host, a dinner at home should proceed more or less in the way described above, perhaps with some minor variations to add interest for your Cambodian guests, many of whom will be familiar with Western ways. If possible, ascertain in advance whether any of your guests are vegetarian or have any other food taboos. Some may eat fish and not meat, for instance. In any event, have a vegetarian option.

Bear in mind that while many Cambodians working with expatriates are fluent in English, their spouses and friends may not be, and conversation can be difficult and limited—but with a carefully devised seating plan, whether you are entertaining them at home or in a restaurant, embarrassment can be avoided. At home, set places at table, with name cards. Bear the above dos and don'ts in mind.

Welcome your Cambodian friends with tea and a selection of drinks, being sure to provide a variety of nonalcoholic drinks, especially for the women. These should be accompanied by nuts and local nibbles taken around and offered on small plates. Remember that food must not be touched with the left hand, so the use of cocktail sticks and little plates will enable guests to pick up the snacks and eat them easily.

The meal itself could be served buffet-style, in which case invite the most prominent person present to go first, and explain the contents of the dishes. If you are serving European food at the table, do so in the Cambodian manner, describing what is in each dish as it arrives, and make sure that rice and spiced sauces are available. Do provide bread as well, as Cambodians, especially of the middle and professional classes, are familiar with European cuisine through the colonial connection.

After the meal, tea and coffee may be served in the sitting room. Cambodians regard coffee as ending both the meal and the evening, and will shortly after this begin to depart, usually awaiting the first move from the most prominent guest. However, attitudes are changing, and relations between Cambodians and their expatriate friends are less formal. A large number of those in business and professional circles have had education and training overseas and have returned with more relaxed social attitudes.

If you are entertaining at a restaurant, consult a colleague or friend with experience and choose an appropriate menu. Make sure to be at the restaurant to greet your guests and to have arranged a place to gather for drinks before going to the table. Name cards should be provided and the guests seated with the oldest preceding the rest. It is polite to order more than they can be expected to eat. Wait for the oldest guest to begin.

HOUSEHOLD HELP

If you are working in Cambodia in a business or professional capacity, you will probably be provided with accommodation, or have it found for you by your employer. If you are in the country for only a short time you may be put up in a hotel, but for an extended length of time you will be provided with a house or an apartment. In that case it is usual to acquire one or more servants, depending on the size of your accommodation and on your lifestyle. You will be expected to have domestic help for cleaning, laundry, and other chores. If you have a house with a garden, you may have a gardener, and depending on your circumstances you may also have a driver.

A single person or a couple in an apartment may manage with one servant, who may live in or come in daily or as required. Families may also employ someone to help look after the children. A house will have domestic quarters attached, and a couple may be employed to do the domestic and gardening chores. Cambodians in the employ of expatriates expect to have a particular job; thus a man might be a gardener or a driver, but not both. If the servant lives away from the house, then he or she must be on call.

Before employing anyone, seek advice from your colleagues. They will have been through the experience and will probably be able to suggest suitable candidates. You may inherit someone who has worked for your predecessor. In any case, word will soon get around that you are looking. Take a little time before making a decision. Seek testimonials, and when you interview candidates have with you a person with some experience and some knowledge of the language. The conditions of service, including the amount of free time and the level of wages, should be commensurate with those of servants employed by your colleagues.

Servants should be clear as to what is expected of them, and should be treated with respect. They will understand their role and will respond more willingly to clear direction and guidance than to direct orders. If a servant should make a mistake, it is more in keeping with Cambodian behavior to show them what you want rather than to be angry, impatient, or critical. Nevertheless, the employer/servant relationship is a personal one, and different individuals will develop different relationships with their staff. Treat them fairly and with consideration while making clear your expectations

Always bear in mind that when employing a servant you are creating a personal relationship, not only with the individual servant but also with his or her family. You will be taking on some responsibility for that family, and may be expected to employ another family member if you need another servant, or to help another family member to find employment with another expatriate. You may also be expected to help if a member of the family needs medical assistance.

chapter six

TIME OUT

As in other countries of the region, Cambodians like to go out in families or groups, often dining out together in the cool of the evening. Cafés and restaurants are full, and some restaurants have live traditional music, which, with traditional dance, is returning to Cambodia after its suppression by the Khmer Rouge.

Sporting activities are popular, particularly those that rely on skill, agility, and a minimum of equipment.

TRADITIONAL CULTURE

As part of their effort to destroy all reminders of the past, the Khmer Rouge targeted Cambodia's traditional arts. Angkor was spared as a symbol of Khmer glory, but all other artistic forms of expression were attacked. Statues, artifacts, and musical instruments were smashed, books were burned, including the contents of the National Library in Phnom Penh, and artists, writers, sculptors, musicians, and anyone associated with the arts were killed or sent into forced labor.

One of the most savage acts was the execution of all but a few of the country's classical dancers, and it took many years to revive that tradition. The Royal University of Fine Arts reestablished the royal ballet only in 1994.

Cambodian classical dance was associated with the royal court, and is similar to the classical dance of India and Thailand. The temples of Angkor have many bas-reliefs portraying female dancers. The dances are stately, and the costumes elaborate and colorful. Great importance is placed on the movement of the hands.

Traditional music, too, has been revived. It was also developed in the court, and is played on traditional instruments such as a three-stringed fiddle, a single-stringed bowed instrument, wind instruments, gongs, xylophones, and drums.

Traditional instruments are played at weddings. Cambodia has its own popular music scene, and you will hear its music and performers on Cambodian radio and television, and live in the larger restaurants.

WATS AND PAGODAS

During your time in Cambodia, you will almost certainly be visiting a Buddhist temple (*pagoda*) or monastery (*wat*). Buddhism is important in the life of Cambodians, and the temples and monasteries, and the monks themselves, are treated with great respect. Whether you are attending a ceremony at the temple, as may well happen if you acquire Cambodian friends, or you are just visiting as a tourist, you should keep the following points in mind.

• Dress modestly, with arms and legs covered.
• Uncover your head. This applies to women as well as men.
• Remove your shoes before entering the temple sanctuary.
• Speak quietly, and be restrained and respectful in your behavior. Observe the behavior of the Cambodian worshipers around you.
• If you sit down in front of a statue of the Buddha, sit with your feet to the side, and not in the lotus position.
• Bow slightly in the presence of elderly or senior monks.

- Don't point your finger or the soles of your feet toward either a statue of the Buddha or a monk.
- Make a small contribution to the donation box; this will be appreciated by the monks and the worshipers.

SPORTS, GAMES, AND OTHER ENTERTAINMENTS

Cambodians engage in sporting activities that are traditional also in other parts of Southeast Asia. Among these are kickboxing and cockfighting. Popular among young men, and requiring skill and agility, is *tapak takraw*, in which teams of four or five kick a rattan ball across a high net. Only the feet may be used, and the game

requires great agility. Ball games introduced from outside, like football, volleyball, and basketball are popular because they need the minimum of equipment, can be played in a relatively confined space, and demand skill and agility rather than brute strength. An annual event is the boat racing during the festival of Bom Om Tuk in early November, marking both the victory of Jayavarman (later Jayavarman VII) over the

Chams and the annual reversal of the waters of the Tonle Sap. Rowing teams from across Cambodia compete, racing in traditional boats.

Prior to the Khmer Rouge regime, attention was being paid to developing Cambodia's participation in international sports and athletics. However, facilities such as the Olympic Stadium and the National Sports Complex in Phnom Penh suffered damage and neglect under the Khmer Rouge. Now restored, they provide facilities for football, tennis, badminton, swimming, and other activities. The good hotels have gymnasiums and swimming pools, and if you are living in Cambodia you will gain access to public facilities and private clubs through your business and social contacts. Golfers are catered for by the Royal Golf Club and the Cambodia Golf and Country Club.

An institution you may find interesting is the Hash House Harriers, an informal running club that meets every Sunday. Largely expatriate, the runners follow a trail laid earlier by two "hares" and having gaps or checks enabling the back runners to catch up while the front runners search for the beginning of the next part of the trail. The run ends with refreshments, mainly beer. It is a good way to meet other expatriates as well as locals and get into expatriate life.

FOOD AND DRINK

Khmer cuisine is similar to Thai, but uses fewer spices. Cooked food is safe to eat because it has been boiled or fried at a high temperature. Rice is the staple food. In Khmer *nam bai* ("eat rice") means, simply, eating. Aside from rice, fish and soup predominate. A fermented fish paste known as *prahoc* is a common and distinctive ingredient of many dishes. A particular specialty is *trey ahng*, which is grilled freshwater fish, wrapped in lettuce or spinach, and served with a fish sauce made with ground

peanuts. Salad dishes are flavored with coriander, mint, and lemongrass. However, note that it is wise to avoid salads when eating out unless you can be assured that they have been washed in boiled water. Popular and cheap are two dishes similar to those in neighboring states. *Bobor* is a rice porridge eaten at any time of day, often with fresh fish and ginger. *Kyteow* is a noodle soup, with a mixture of ingredients, which makes a spicy and satisfying meal. *Samlor* (soup) is popular, and among the favorites are *samlor machou banle* (hot and sour fish soup with pineapple and spices), *samlor chapek* (pork soup flavored with ginger), *samlor ktis* (fish soup with ginger and pineapple), and *Samlor machou bawng kawng*, a prawn soup similar to the Thai *tom yam*. Other delicacies include frog, turtle, and fried crickets and tarantula.

The French have left a legacy of freshly baked bread, so one can have coffee and croissants. Favorite local desserts are sticky rice cakes and jackfruit pudding. There is a range of local fruits including bananas, rambutans, pineapples, mangoes, mangosteens, jackfruit, and the strong-smelling durian, regarded by some as an aphrodisiac. Make sure that all fruits you buy are unpeeled, and peel them yourself.

Drinks

Tap water is unsafe to drink. Throughout Cambodia ice is produced from treated water and is thus safe, but you may still wish to avoid ice in drinks unless you can be sure that it has been made from boiled water. Mineral water, bottled soft drinks, and beer are safe to drink, as are tea and coffee, where the water will have been boiled. Tea, served without milk or sugar, accompanies every meal.

Fruit smoothies, called *tikalok*, are widely available, and in rural areas sugar palm juice is a traditional thirst quencher. Femented, it becomes an alcoholic beverage. Beer is a popular drink, and there are a number of local and foreign brands. Wines from Australia and Europe are relatively cheap, as are both local and imported spirits.

TWO WARNINGS

- When buying mineral water, check that the cap is secure. It can happen that street sellers refill empty bottles with tap water.
- Brush your teeth with boiled water.

EATING OUT

If you are in the country for some time, your introduction to the local cuisine and restaurants will almost certainly come through Cambodian contacts, or through expatriates who have acquired local knowledge. They will tell you about the best places. If you are on a short visit, and staying in a hotel, ask the information clerk where to eat and drink outside the hotel. Or just walk out and look for a place with a crowd of people dining in it—always a sign that the food will be good.

There are numerous eating places serving a variety of cuisines—Khmer, Chinese, Thai, Vietnamese, Japanese, French, Italian, and Indian and Bangladeshi—and ranging from street stalls and small, family-run businesses to upscale international-style restaurants in converted colonial villas or large hotels. Popular places for eating out are the riverside areas of Phnom Penh and Siem Reap, and the beach resorts, as at Sihanoukville; but each city and town has its lesser equivalents. Even in the rural areas the smaller centers will have a café, bar, or stall where tasty traditional food is served and the locals eat and drink. For good food and good value, try the street stalls and small street-side cafés, from

which you can observe the people and life around you. For more formal indoor or terrace venues you pay more, and of course the international restaurants in the hotels, which impose tax and service, are expensive, especially by Cambodian standards.

Even in the smaller establishments menus may be bilingual, the second language usually being English, though occasionally the English version may still need deciphering. If there is no English and you don't know the Khmer word yourself, point to the items on display to order your choices.

Tourism has resulted in a Western-style fast-food sector, especially in the main tourist centers.

> ### TIPPING
> The more expensive hotels and restaurants impose a 10 percent service charge. Just a small tip or a request to "keep the change" will be welcome in restaurants and bars.
>
> Drivers and guides should receive a tip for their time and effort.
>
> If you are staying at a hotel for any length of time, leave a tip for those who clean the room. Tipping is not necessarily expected elsewhere.

BARS AND NIGHTCLUBS

If you are in Cambodia on a long visit, your Cambodian and expatriate contacts and colleagues will, if you wish, introduce you to the nightlife in the area that caters to an adult clientele and stays open until midnight or later.

There are numerous late-night bars, in which bottled and canned beers are the most popular drinks, the local brand being Angkor. There are nightclubs in Phnom Penh, Siem Reap, Sihanoukville, and tourist areas. Traditionally, Cambodian women avoided drinking alcohol and only recently have single Cambodian women begun frequenting bars. The girls serving in the bars and clubs are usually from poorer backgrounds, many of them from rural areas. They offer companionship, dancing partnership, and other services. Cambodians often prefer to think that they are Vietnamese.

PHOTOGRAPHY

If you want to take photographs or videos of people, ask them politely if they will allow this. Respect their right to privacy, though, and show particular respect toward monks and worshipers. Cambodians are courteous and will usually agree to have their photograph taken if they are asked in the right way. The digital camera, with its capacity to show the image taken on its viewing screen, makes it possible to show the result immediately, and children will usually be delighted with this, especially in the rural areas. They may actually ask to be photographed, especially if they can then see themselves on the screen.

SHOPPING FOR PLEASURE

If you are looking for attractive mementos of your stay, there is a wide choice in Phnom Penh and Siem Reap, ranging from souvenirs aimed at the tourist market—to be found in the coastal resorts and in any place tourists visit—to high-quality items including old and new objects of various kinds, such as antiques, textiles, old coins or swords, silver, paintings, sculptures, wood carvings, and so on. There are upscale shops, some in the more expensive hotels, which cater to the affluent collector or tourist, and numerous smaller establishments and market stalls.

Bargaining

Remember that Cambodians appreciate some bargaining, but not the ferocious attempts to knock down prices that is the custom in some cultures. An apparent reluctance to buy will usually produce a lower offer, often from an inflated stated price, even in the best shops. However, in the markets and in smaller shops, the asking price will not usually be overinflated and good-natured bargaining will usually produce a quick result. Cambodians are not wealthy, and the difference in the asking price and a fair price is of less consequence to you than to them. If you are living or working in the country, take some time to establish values, consulting with both expatriate and Cambodian colleagues as to what constitutes a fair price.

Antiques

The years of conflict led to the destruction and loss of many genuine antique artifacts in Cambodia, but many were spared. However, the genuine article is more likely to be found in a reputable antique shop than on a market stall. Cambodian craftsmen are skilled at reproducing copies of antique objects and, as in other parts of the world, the more unscrupulous have mastered the techniques for "aging" items so that they appear genuine. Inevitably fakes are passed off as antiques, usually as Angkorian or Chinese pieces, and if the deal seems too good to be true, it probably is. If you are tempted to buy something of which you are unsure of the provenance, seek advice. Nevertheless, there are some interesting and beautiful objects available, and if you have seen something that you can acquire for an acceptable price to yourself, it is of course up to you whether you like it enough, whatever its provenance, to buy it as a souvenir of your visit.

Sandstone Carvings
Do not attempt to take sandstone carvings from the Angkorian and pre-Angkorian periods out of Cambodia. This is illegal.

Paintings
These range from often poor-quality pictures with an Angkorian theme to more exciting contemporary works that may be found in the art shops of Phnom Penh and Siem Reap, and in galleries in the upscale hotels. If you are spending some time in Cambodia, you will have

opportunities to get into the local art scene and purchase new and fresh works, which are exhibited in a wide range of techniques and styles.

Sculpture

Sculpture is one of the most prominent art forms of Angkor, so it is not surprising that skilled stone carvers flourish in Cambodia today, producing replicas of ancient works for the tourist market. Alongside them are those who produce original work on more contemporary themes. You may not be able to carry home a large piece of sculpture, but there are smaller pieces that make attractive souvenirs. Remember that it is illegal to take out a genuine Angkorian stone sculpture.

Silver

Cambodian silver is renowned for its beauty and the fine detail of its craftsmanship. However, silver needs an alloy to give it strength, and the silver content of pieces for sale ranges from the insignificant through 50 percent to almost pure silver. It can be difficult to tell the difference and be sure of what you are buying. A reputable shop should tell you the percentage of silver to alloy in its pieces; market sellers may not.

Textiles

Textiles are ideal souvenirs in that they can be easily packed. Cambodia is particularly noted for its silk, much of it handwoven and dyed using natural dyes. The best silk comes from the

provinces of Kampong Cham and Takeo. You can buy it from Artisans d'Angkor, which is based in Siem Reap and has branches in Phnom Penh, including at Psar Tuol Tom Pong and at the international airports. High-quality silk is also produced at Stung Treng and Joom Noon in Theng Meanchey province. Silk is also imported from China and Vietnam, so look for the genuine Cambodian article.

Wood Carving

This is another popular and highly skilled craft. Subjects include images of Buddha, carvings of Angkorian statues, betel nut boxes—that is, finely carved boxes for carrying the betel nut and the instruments for preparing it—inlaid jewelry boxes, carved animal figures, and elaborately decorated wheels used in weaving. Such items can be found in shops and markets, and it is best to look about before making a decision.

Furniture

It is possible to buy beautifully handcrafted furniture. If you will be resident for some time you may enjoy buying pieces with the intention of taking them home when your stay is over.

Clothes

Cambodia produces clothing for a number of
international brands. Look in the upscale
boutique-style shops, the large stores, clothing
and textile shops in the bazaars, and the markets,
especially Psar Tuol Tom Pong (see below).

Markets (*Psar*)

The main market in Phnom Penh is the Psar
Thiem, also known as the Central Market. It's
housed under a huge dome with four wings and
filled with all kinds
of goods from gold
to clothing. Stop
for refreshment at
one of the many
food and drink
stalls, and watch
the world go by.

Psar Tuol Tom Pong is the best market for
shopping for everything from souvenirs, crafts,
silk, textiles, and antiques, both real and faked,
and is very popular with tourists. It is called the
Russian Market because the Russians shopped
there during the 1980s.

Psar O Russel has nothing to do with Russians.
It is located in what appears to be a shopping
mall, but there are hundreds of stalls, again selling
all kinds of goods. Psar Olympic and Psar Chaa
are also large indoor markets worth visiting.

chapter seven

TRAVEL, HEALTH, & SAFETY

Cambodia's infrastructure was badly damaged during the years of conflict. However, much has been repaired and upgraded, and moving around the country by air, land, and water is largely trouble free.

Passport and visa requirements for entry are straightforward. You will need a valid passport expiring no sooner than six months from your planned departure date. Tourist visas for one month are obtainable on arrival at the airports at Phnom Penh and Siem Reap and at the border crossing from neighboring states, and can be renewed for one month only. Carry a passport-sized photograph with you to be attached to the visa. Business visas cost more but can be extended for longer periods.

Be aware, however, that entry and visa requirements may change. Contact the Cambodian Embassy in your home country for current requirements, or consult your travel agent.

ARRIVAL
The easiest way to enter Cambodia is to fly from Bangkok to either Siem Reap or Phnom Penh. Scheduled flights fly to Phnom Penh from Kuala

Lumpur, Singapore, Ho Chi Minh City, Vientiane, Hong Kong, and Guangzhou. Budget airlines also link Phnom Penh with Bangkok, Kuala Lumpur, and Singapore. The airport at Phnom Penh is four miles (7 km) from the city, and taxis are relatively cheap, particularly if you are prepared to share.

Land border crossings are mainly for the adventurous traveler. The road from the Thai border at Siem Reap is being upgraded. One can travel by ferry and bus from Thailand's Trat Province to the Cambodian coastal town of Krong Koh Kong. Buses and shared taxis take passengers to Vietnam's entry point to Cambodia at Moc Bai. Visas can be obtained at the border crossings. Currently the land border with Laos is closed.

TRAVEL WITHIN THE COUNTRY
By Road

Cambodia's road system suffered badly from neglect during the years of conflict. Much has been done with international aid in the past few years to develop the major roads and upgrade them to expressways where appropriate, as between Phnom Penh and Sihanoukville and from Phnom Penh to Siem Reap and Battambang.

Cars and motorcycles are available for rent. Almost all car rentals include a driver, which, given the state of the roads and the behavior on them, is reassuring. If you wish to drive yourself, you should have an international driver's license. No license is required for renting a motorcycle. If you are working in Cambodia or staying for any length of time and intend to drive, then a Cambodian license will be required, but many expatriates employ their own drivers.

Conditions on the road can be chaotic. Traffic in Cambodia drives on the right-hand side of the road, as in the United States or continental Europe. However, this is loosely interpreted. Many

Cambodians have never taken a driving test and their driving skills and knowledge of traffic rules are variable. More importantly, much of the road traffic is slow. Bicycles and pedlos (bicycles adapted to create a three-wheeled pedaled vehicle to carry a passenger) are used to carry not only the rider but often surprisingly large loads. At the next level is the "moto," a small motorbike that is used to its utmost capacity to carry passengers, frequently a whole family perched before and behind the driver. Motos are often converted to carry large loads by having a shelf attached behind the rider, or a trailer. They are unlicensed, yet their owners compete to perform a taxi service, picking up passengers at the curbside and weaving through the traffic to their destination. The cars on the roads include a large proportion of taxis, manned by drivers determined to get the journey over quickly in order to pick up the next passenger.

Motorists have to get through the jumble of slower traffic and keep an eye open for faster and nippier motorcyclists who weave in and out and often cut across from one side of the road to the other. In the rural areas there are also hazards caused by wandering people and animals.

A car is useful for getting around Phnom Penh and Siem Reap, and gives you the freedom to take your time at places of interest. However, it is safer and less stressful to hire a vehicle and driver. If you intend to travel out of town or tour more widely the costs are higher and you will need to pay for the driver's accommodation and food as well as your own. Gas prices are significantly higher in the countryside.

Motorcycles can also be rented in Phnom Penh and other towns, but riders should be aware of the hazardous traffic conditions there, and note that traveling in this way in the countryside is not recommended for the novice.

Buses

Bus travel has improved with the roads, and modern, air-conditioned coaches provide regular services between Phnom Penh and the other major cities and towns, including Siem Reap, Battambang, Takeo, Kampong Cham, and Kampot. Phnom Penh Public Transport is the oldest and largest company. Mekong Express offers more luxurious travel to Siem Reap and Battambang.

Services are regular, and fares are cheap. You can buy tickets from hotels and street kiosks. Either the coach will pick you up from where you bought your tickets, or a minibus will do so and transport you to the bus terminus to board the coach. Tickets are numbered, so there is no overcrowding.

Minibuses also operate, but they do not keep a regular schedule and leave when full. If they have air-conditioning it may be inefficient. Their use has declined as coaches have drawn off customers, but if you have the time to use them, and wish to meet ordinary Cambodians, you will enjoy doing so.

Rail Travel

Cambodia's rail system also has suffered from neglect and consists of about 400 miles (645 km) of single-track meter gauge line, much of it poorly maintained. Trains travel at an average of around 12 mph (20 kmph). The line to Sihanoukville passes through Takeo and Kampot, a total of 143 miles (228 km). That to the northwest links Phnom Penh with Puirsat, Battambang, and Sisophon, a total of 188 miles (302 km). Cambodia is beginning to upgrade its rail system with assistance from its ASEAN partners. Traveling by train is a good way to see some spectacular scenery and to meet people, who will be curious about you. It is likely that someone will have enough English to speak to you.

Boat Travel

Cambodia has 1,180 miles (1,900km) of navigable waterways. Express boats operate between Phnom

Penh and Siem Reap. These are overcrowded and uncomfortable compared with the coach services, but the journey takes less time—about three to five hours, depending on the size and power of the boat. There are also slower and cheaper services. The route between Phnom Penh and Siem Reap crosses the vast expanse of the Tonle Sap, which is not particularly picturesque, but the route is popular with locals and tourists. Boat services up the Mekong depart from Kampong Cham, which is accessible by road from Phnom Penh. Travel along the Mekong by boat is more scenic, and at Kratie you may see freshwater dolphins. There is also an attractive river route between Siem Reap and Battambang.

Air Travel

There are several regular daily flights between Phnom Penh and Siem Reap, and flights also from Phnom Penh to regional capitals, though domestic airlines have had difficulties and it will be necessary to find out the current situation at the time you wish to travel. Check the situation with your travel agent either when you are planning your trip to Cambodia, or after your arrival in the country. There is a small domestic airport tax.

HEALTH AND MEDICAL CARE

Cambodia's health services suffered under the Khmer Rouge. Despite government efforts, which are continuing to bring improvement, they are still of variable standard. Good medical facilities are available in Phnom Penh and Siem Reap, but the countryside is still poorly served. If you are taken ill while you are outside those centers, you should return to them for treatment. If your medical condition is serious you may be sent to Bangkok.

Medical Care

Despite taking all sensible precautions you may fall ill or suffer an injury that requires medical attention. If you are living and working in Cambodia, you will have access to medical care arranged by or through your employer, or you can seek advice from your employer, colleagues, or friends with local knowledge. If you are on vacation you should have medical insurance to cover the expenses you may incur, but you will need to pay up-front and in cash before you can file a claim. Those who have a condition requiring special medication should bring a sufficient supply for their whole time in Cambodia; however, pharmacies carry a wide range of medicines for most common ailments.

The best medical facilities are in Phnom Penh and Siem Reap. Away from those centers, local government facilities are often rather primitive and you might have difficulty making yourself understood there. Therefore, if you will be traveling outside the main centers, seek advice from a good hotel or an embassy or consulate and obtain the names and locations of individual local doctors and clinics near the places you will be traveling. If you  are with a group, the tour operator will have the necessary information.

Like all tropical countries, Cambodia is home to diseases and infections that are less prevalent and more easily treated in the cities. Greater caution has to be observed if traveling in the rural areas. Travelers in such areas should carry medicine and first-aid equipment with them and take all available preventive measures. On an organized tour the risks will be slight and advice will be available.

The list of health risks given below appears daunting, but Cambodia is no less safe than any other country in the region if you stay within reasonable bounds, observe elementary hygiene, and take all necessary precautions.

Hepatitis is endemic. There are six types of viral hepatitis with similar symptoms. These include a general lassitude and physical debilitation accompanied by fever, headaches, chills, general aches and pains, nausea, vomiting, dark urine, light-colored feces, jaundiced skin, and yellowing of the whites of the eyes.

Hepatitis A and E can cause acute illness, but there is a vaccine and you will recover. Rest, drink plenty of fluids, eat lightly, and avoid fatty foods.

Hepatitis A and E are transmitted via fecal-oral contact and are a product of unsanitary conditions. Elementary hygiene reduces risk.

Hepatitis B and D have similar symptoms to types A and E, but type B can be more severe and can lead to long-term liver damage, liver cancer, and the risk of being a long-term carrier. Both types are transmitted via blood, saliva, semen, and vaginal fluids. A vaccine is available.

Hepatitis C is transmitted only by blood-to-blood contact. At the time of writing there is no vaccine. Type G hepatitis is not dangerous.

Malaria is spread by mosquitoes and is potentially fatal. In areas where it is endemic, take antimalarial tablets and try to avoid being bitten. Wear long-sleeved shirts and long trousers, especially in the evenings, use mosquito coils, and sleep under mosquito nets. The symptoms include fever, headache, chills and sweating, diarrhea, abdominal pains, and a general feeling of illness. Medication is available.

There are various forms of malaria. Check with your health provider as to which medication is needed for where you are going. Should you contract malaria and respond to treatment, remember that the malaria parasite may persist even though symptoms have gone. Be retested for malaria to see that it does not recur.

Typhoid is transmitted via food and water and is an enteric disease caused by a type of salmonella bacteria. Early symptoms are similar to influenza, with fever, headache, loss of appetite, and a general feeling of illness. You may experience constipation or diarrhea. Fever and headache may become more severe and a red skin rash and sore throat may develop. Jaundice can be another symptom. Typhoid can be confused with malaria, but with typhoid the pulse rate is relatively slow for a person with fever. About 10 percent of cases become serious and it is advisable to seek medical advice as soon as any of the above symptoms occur.

Rabies is a fatal viral infection transmitted through the saliva of furry animals such as dogs, cats, bats, and monkeys, and is not dependent on a bite. It may pass through the saliva into a cut or scratch—made by the animal or already present. If you are licked or bitten by such an animal, clean the area promptly and thoroughly with soap and running water, and disinfectant, alcohol, or iodine, and seek immediate medical attention. A course of injections will prevent the onset of symptoms.

Japanese B Encephalitis is a mosquito-borne infection of the brain that occurs in the rural rice-growing areas. Travelers are at low risk. There is a vaccine, but take precautions against mosquito bites as outlined above in the note on malaria.

SAFETY
Don't wander off the beaten track. Unexploded ordnance—shells, mortars, rockets, bombs, mines, and other war material—is a possible hazard.

Cambodia has done much to eradicate the problem, but it is estimated that there are from four to six million unexploded mines littering the countryside. All main roads have been cleared,

but do not depart from them. If you are in a remote area, keep to the road or track, and seek advice before traveling. If you are living in the country you will soon become aware of the problem and of the precautions to take when traveling to places of interest. The main tourist sites are safe, but keep within their boundaries.

The years of conflict have left many guns in undesirable hands. Gun crime is not as common as might be expected, but travelers are warned to be cautious, especially at night and in rural areas. Motorcycle thefts and holdups are more likely in Phnom Penh and Sihanoukville than elsewhere. Walking and riding alone late at night is not advisable. However, as in any other country, there is little danger if sensible precautions are taken.

Tourists may become the targets of pickpockets, but, again, simple precautions can reduce the likelihood. Don't leave belongings unattended, and keep money and valuables safely out of sight.

PLACES TO VISIT

There are many reasons to visit Cambodia. The main one is to see the glories of its past—particularly the ruins of Angkor, but also other sites in various parts of the country that speak of its history—but its natural beauty, wildlife, coastal islands, and beaches are further attractions.

Cambodians are proud of their heritage, especially of that left of the great Khmer empire centered on Angkor. This was the one part of Cambodia's heritage that was not attacked and desecrated, the Khmer Rouge retaining it as a symbol of Khmer pride and identity. With the passing of the Khmer Rouge regime, the old arts have been revived. Linked to the commercialism that inevitably accompanies tourism is pride in their ancient past, just as there is shame for their more recent experiences under the Khmer Rouge. It is significant that they have retained the scenes of atrocity as memorials to the depths to which Cambodia sank, in the hope that such things may never happen again.

Phnom Penh

Phnom Penh, despite recent history, retains a charm based on its royal and colonial past. The

French left a legacy of colonial architecture that still provides a pleasing backdrop to the busy street life, now reinforced by redevelopment of the waterfront, which is especially lively on Friday and Saturday nights. Phnom Penh has quite a large Chinese population, and Chinese New Year is a good time to see dragon dances in the streets.

As the royal capital after the move from Angkor, the city possesses a number of impressive *wats* and palaces. The Silver Pagoda is the most spectacular temple, and was preserved by the Khmer Rouge as a repository of Khmer culture. Among the other *wats* of importance are Wat Ounalon, Wat Phnom, and Wat Moha Montrei.

Sihanoukville
Sihanoukville (Kampong Saom), the port city on the southern coast, also offers white sandy beaches, access to unspoiled tropical islands, excellent fresh seafood, and an active nightlife. It is served by an international airport.

The Killing Fields of Choeung Ek

A white stupa marks the location of 125 mass graves, forty-three of which remain untouched, and is a memorial to the 17,000 people executed here by the Khmer Rouge between mid-1975 and December 1978. Displayed on shelves behind the stupa's glass panels are the skulls of 8,000 victims, many of them bludgeoned to death to save bullets. This was not the only place of execution, but remains as a symbol and a memorial to all those who died in similar circumstances.

Phnom Sontuk

Situated in Cambodia's northwest, this holy mountain is adorned with pagodas and statues of the Buddha. Rising high above the surrounding countryside, it is approached by a forest path with 980 steps, arriving at a colorful pagoda with many small shrines. Images of the Buddha have been carved into large sandstone boulders. Beneath the southern summit lie generations of reclining Buddhas, the oldest carved into the rock centuries ago, some of the more recent images cast in cement. The monks at the *wat* on the mountain are pleased to welcome tourists.

Kampong Thom, midway between Phnom Penh and Siem Reap, is worth using as a base from which to visit both Phnom Sontuk and the pre-Angkorian temples associated with the Chenla capital of Sambor Prei Kuk. Tours can be arranged from there.

Kirirom National Park

Set in highland pine forests, this area offers good walking trails and sightings of many small waterfalls. You can hire a guide for the two-hour ascent of Phnom Dat Chivit (End of the World Mountain) to the edge of a sheer cliff for a splendid view of the western mountain ranges.

Bokor National Park

Located in the southern tip of the Elephant Mountains, this park has a cool climate. It was formerly a French colonial hill station: a road was first made in 1925 and the hill resort was established at 3,543 feet (1,080 m). The French left in the late 1940s, and it was abandoned to the Khmer Rouge in the early 1970s; it did not fully recover its former status, and retains—but with a colonial charm—the feel of a ghost town. There are several waterfalls, panoramic views to the ocean, and wild animals, including tigers and elephants—though visitors are unlikely to see these.

Siem Reap

Most people visiting or working in Cambodia visit Siem Reap, the gateway to the ruins of Angkor. The town itself retains much of its French colonial charm, with a pleasant riverfront, tree-lined boulevards, and busy shop-houses, with cafés and restaurants. New development sits alongside the old, and tourism has forced up prices. Nevertheless, its proximity to the splendors of Angkor makes it worth it.

The Temples of Angkor

A visit to Angkor is a must for all visitors to Cambodia. Its temples and palaces represent the height of classic Khmer civilization, and demonstrate its wealth and power, its artistic, architectural, and engineering achievements, and the hubris that caused its eventual collapse. Glorifying its rulers and their conquests, the carved temple friezes show battles against the Thais and the Chams and the procedures of government, ritual, war, and justice. One depicts the torture chambers of Hell, and presumably those of the king, indicating that the events of recent years reflected a dark side of Khmer governance and society that had not previously been unknown. Also present are images reflecting the beauty, grace, and culture of the court, the religious contemplation of its inhabitants, the occupations of its people, and the expression of its faiths. Less immediately obvious, except in the lakes and channels still visible, is the skill of the hydraulic engineers of the time, who produced a water supply and irrigation system depending on minute differences in levels, accurately measured to enable the constant flow of the water upon which the life of this great civilization depended.

Admission Passes

One can no longer wander around at will. Visitors must obtain a pass, which can be bought at the entrance booth on the way to Angkor Wat, which allows access to all the main temples within the Siem Reap Angkor area. Passes are available for one day, three days, or a week, and cannot be extended. A multiday pass requires a passport-size photograph, so bring one with you or be prepared to stand in line for an instant photograph. Uniformed guards check the tickets at the main attractions, but are not at the smaller temples. However, you will have to pay a fine if you are found in a temple complex without a pass.

Be sure to check what your pass covers, as some of the remoter attractions are not included. Passes bought after 5:00 p.m. are valid from the following day. No pass is required to visit villages.

Moving Around the Site

There are numerous ways of getting around to see the temples, and your choice may depend on the number traveling together, the weather, your fitness, and the time and money you have to spend.

• *Minibus.* Tours operate out of Siem Reap.
• *Car, cyclo, pedicab.* You can rent a car with a driver

to take you around the circuit. For some of the less accessible temples you can rent a 4WD. A cyclo or pedicab will be slower than a car, but all offer some protection from the weather.

- *Motorcycle.* Known as "motos," these may be rented with a driver, the tourist sitting behind. They can be rented in Phnom Penh, but not in Siem Reap. Be aware of the speed restrictions, which are there to protect other users. The drivers are generally knowledgeable, and will drop you off and pick you up as required. You can also get a moto from one temple to another.
- *Remorque-moto.* This is a moto with a small covered carriage for two people towed behind.
- *Helicopter.* Helicopter Cambodia offers a spectacular but expensive way to view the temples from the air, or to fly to the more remote temples.
- *Hot-air balloon.* This is a tethered balloon that rises to 656 feet (200 m) and provides a fine aerial view for up to thirty people.
- *Elephant.* A chance to go back in time! The ride is from the south gate of Angkor Thom to the Bayon in the morning, and to the summit of Phnom Bakheng for sunset.
- *On foot.* You can walk to Angkor Thom and to Angkor Wat from Siem Reap, and this is a good way to meet people and see the sites up close.
- *Bicycle.* In many respects, this is the best choice. You can see and hear without obstruction, the area is relatively flat, you can stop where you like, and spend as much time as you like. It also brings you closer to the ordinary people you may meet.

THE TEMPLE COMPLEX OF ANGKOR

The following is a list of the major sites at Angkor within easy reach of Siem Reap. Once in Cambodia you will be able to obtain a detailed map of all the sites at Angkor, and any tourist office or hotel will have further information. There are, of course, guidebooks devoted to the temples, and these pages set out to describe only the main scenes and events depicted on the walls of the most important temples. There is in most cases a sequence of images, which makes the story clear, and this is worth understanding before a first visit.

Angkor Wat

Probably built by King Suryavarman II (1112–52) both to honor Vishnu and as his own mausoleum, the temple is oriented to the west, the direction associated with Vishnu and with death. It is the largest and best preserved of the temples at Angkor, and is believed to be the biggest religious site in the world. The whole complex is a replication of the Hindu universe. The central tower represents Mount Meru, rising over the lower peaks represented by the lower towers. The courtyards are the continents and the outer moat the oceans. The seven-headed *naga* serpent represents the rainbow bridge between man and heaven. The dimensions are such that in walking across the causeway to the main entrance and then continuing through the successive courtyards to the central tower, one metaphorically travels back in time to the creation of the universe. Each stage represents one of the four ages of classical Hindu thought.

The huge scale of the structure is awesome. The moat is 620 feet (190 m) wide and forms a rectangle measuring 1.18 miles (1.5 km) by 0.94 miles (1.3 km). The stone for the temple was quarried more than thirty miles (50 km) away and carried down the Siem Reap River on rafts before being manhandled into position. The main entrance is through a large and richly decorated porch 856 feet (258 m) wide on the western side. In a gate tower to the right is a large statue of Vishnu, which is still revered.

From the entrance a long, broad avenue leads to the main temple. It is lined with *naga* balustrades and passes between two libraries and two pools before arriving at the entrance to the central temple. This is built on three levels, which enclose a square surrounded by interlinked galleries. The Gallery of a Thousand Buddhas is one of these; but it now greatly depleted and the remaining statues are severely damaged.

The second and third stories have towers at
their corners, and from the middle rises the great
central tower. The central sanctuary once housed
a gold stature of Vishnu riding a *garuda*, part
man, part bird, which represented the deified
god-king Suryavarman II. The stairs to this upper
level are extremely steep and should be climbed
with great caution. Once at the summit, however,
pause, relax, and absorb the amazing view and the
sense of wonder this great monument evokes.

At ground level, further wonder awaits you.
The vast inner wall of the cloister surrounding the
lower level is covered with bas-reliefs, the great
majority dating from the twelfth century, with
some added in the sixteenth. Starting at the
western wall, and keeping the wall to your left,
you will see the following in turn.

a) *The Battle of Kurukshetra*
On the southern wall of the west gallery is
depicted a scene from the Hindu epic

Mahabharata. The Kauravas, coming from the left, meet the Pandavas, coming from the right. Infantry are shown on the lowest tier, with officers on elephants and chiefs on the second and third tiers. The carving is detailed and clear, and highly polished by being touched by millions of hands. Individual incidents can be seen.

b) *The Army of Suryavarman II*
The western section of the south gallery shows the army of Suryavarman II. The king, wearing a coronet and carrying a battle-axe, is seated on an elephant; he is shaded by fifteen umbrellas and fanned by servants. Then there are officers and chiefs on horseback, among them chiefs on elephants. The Khmer soldiers wear square

breastplates and carry spears. Further on is a depiction of the supporting Thai mercenary army, less well-ordered, wearing long headdresses and skirts and carrying tridents.

c) *Heaven and Hell*

The eastern half of the south gallery depicts the rewards of the thirty-seven heavens and the punishments of the thirty-two hells. On the left, the upper and middle tiers show gentlemen and ladies processing toward an eighteen-armed Yama, judge of the dead, seated on a hill, with his assistants, Dharma and Sitragupta, below him. On the lower level is the road to hell, along which the wicked are dragged by devils. To Yama's right the tableau is divided horizontally by a line of *garuda*, the upper level depicting heaven, where the elect dwell in beautiful mansions served by servants, women, and children, while below the condemned suffer the tortures of hell.

d) *The Churning of the Sea of Milk*

The southern section of the east gallery depicts

the Churning of the Sea of Milk. Beautifully executed, this relief depicts eighty-eight *asura* (demons) on the left and ninety-two *deva* (gods) to the right churning up the sea of milk in order to extract the elixir of immortality that both desire. The demons hold the head of the serpent and the gods the tail. At the center, the serpent is coiled around Mount Mandala, which in the tug-of-war is turned and churns up the sea. Vishnu, incarnated as a giant turtle, lends his shell as the base and pivot upon which Mount Mandala turns. Present also are Brahma, Shiva, Hanuman, the monkey god, and Lakshmi, goddess of beauty. Above, a host of *apsaras* (heavenly nymphs) sing and dance, encouraging the gods and distracting the demons.

e) *Elephant Gate*
This gate, which has no stairs leading to it, was used by the king and others of rank to mount and dismount from elephants directly from the gallery.

f) *Vishnu Conquering the Demons*
The northern section of the east gallery depicts a furious battle between Vishnu, mounted on a *garuda*, and a horde of *danava* (demons), who are getting the worst of it. Carved probably in the sixteenth century, this is inferior to the earlier reliefs.

g) *Krishna and the Demon King*
The eastern section of the north gallery depicts Vishnu incarnated as Krishna mounted on a *garuda* before a burning walled city, the residence of the demon king Bana. The *garuda* puts out the fire and Bana is captured. In the final scene, Krishna kneels before Shiva and asks that Bana's life be spared.

h) *The Battle of the Gods and the Demons*
The western section of the north gallery depicts a battle between the twenty-one gods of the Hindu

pantheon and various demons. The gods are recognizable by their traditional attributes and mounts. For example, Vishnu has four arms and is mounted on a *garuda*, while Shiva rides a sacred goose.

i) *The Battle of Lanka*

The northern half of the west gallery depicts scenes from the *Ramayana*. In the battle of Lanka, Rama, on the shoulder of Hanuman, along with his army of monkeys battles the ten-headed Ravana, seducer of Rama's wife, Sita. Ravana rides in a chariot drawn by monsters and commands an army of giants.

Angkor Thom

Built by Angkor's greatest king, Jayavarman VII (1181–1219), Angkor Thom replaced the previous Khmer capital sacked by the Chams. A fortified city, it is enclosed by a square wall 26 feet (8 m) high and 7.75 miles (12 km) in length, and circled by a moat 328 feet (100 m) wide, said to have been inhabited by crocodiles. The city has five monumental gates, one in each of the northern, western, and southern walls and two in the eastern wall. The gates are 66 feet (20 m) high, decorated with stone elephant trunks and crowned with four gigantic faces of the Bodhisattva Avalokiteshvara facing the cardinal directions: this is a Buddhist city, not Hindu, even though its design echoes the concept of Mount Meru surrounded by the oceans. The temple at its center is the Bayon, and this is a Buddhist monument. Yet, outside the gates, the balustrades of the causeways over the moat replicate the Churning of the Sea of Milk with fifty-four gods to the left of the causeway and fifty-four demons to the right. The south gate has been restored, and being on the main road into Angkor from Siem Reap is very busy. The east and west gates are more peaceful and are accessible.

Bayon

At the center of Angkor Thom lies the Bayon, which as well as replicating Mount Meru is a grand expression of Jayavarman VII's power and majesty. In form it is a large platform with three levels, the top level supporting fifty-four towers bearing 216 huge faces of Avalokiteshvara, enigmatic and smiling, representing the presence of the king—powerful, but benign, and always present. Oriented to the east, it is often visited in the morning, but it is magnificent at any time and best experienced in relative solitude.

The temple is on three levels. The first two levels are square and adorned with bas-reliefs. The third level is circular and has the towers and the faces. There are 0.744 miles (1.2 km) of bas-reliefs, the most outstanding being those on the first level. If you enter the Bayon by the eastern gate and move clockwise around the first level, the panels are in the following sequence.

a) *The Defeat of the Chams*
Of the three tiers, the lowest shows Khmer soldiers marching to battle with elephants and ox carts. The middle tier shows coffins being carried from the battlefield. The third tier depicts Jayavarman VII on horseback, shaded by parasols and with a retinue of concubines.

b) *Worshiping the Linga*
The first panel north of the southeastern corner shows Hindus praying to a phallic symbol, the *linga*. This image may have originally been a Buddha, later modified by a Hindu king.

c) *Naval Battle on the Tonle Sap*
The sequence contains graphic images of the naval battle fought against the Chams, whose heads are covered, and also scenes of everyday life and the preparation and serving of the feast that celebrated the Khmer victory. Note the crocodiles in the lake waiting for their victims.

d) The last section of the south gallery depicts a military procession, a scene of elephants being brought in from the mountains, and a humorous scene of Brahmans being chased up two trees by tigers.

e) A series of scenes appears to depict a civil war, beginning with groups of people confronting each other and escalating into a general conflict with soldiers and elephants.

f) *The All-Seeing King*
The next panel also shows fighting. In another image a large fish swallows an antelope. Among the smaller fish is a prawn under which an inscription proclaims that the king will seek out those in hiding.

g) A victory parade, with the king carrying a bow.

h) The panel at the western corner of the northern wall depicts a circus. Among the performers is a strongman holding three dwarfs, a man on his back spinning a wheel with his feet, and a group of tightrope walkers. The royal court watches from a terrace, and below is a procession of animals.

i) Two rivers, both teeming with fish.

j) *Battle scenes*
The rest of the north wall carries extensive battle scenes between the Chams and the Khmers. The first shows the defeat and expulsion of the Chams, the second the Cham army advancing, and the third the Chams in pursuit of fleeing Khmers. The story is continued on the northern panels of the eastern wall, where the Chams are shown sacking Angkor, the wounded king being lowered from the back of an elephant, and a wounded Khmer general being

carried in a hammock suspended from a pole, while the Chams pursue the fleeing Khmers.

k) The final panel depicts another meeting of the two armies, the flags of the Chams being a distinctive feature.

The reliefs on the second level of the Bayon are not as spectacular as those on the first level, and do not make up as clear a sequence, but they are well worth viewing.

Terrace of the Leper King

The twelfth-century Terrace of the Leper King is a twenty-three-foot (7-m) high platform that takes its name from a nude but sexless statue. The significance of this figure is unclear; one view is that it represents a Khmer king who had leprosy, another that it represents Yama, the god of death. In either case it is possible that the terrace marks the site where the king was cremated.

The front retaining walls of the terrace are

adorned with five tiers of exquisitely carved seated *apsaras*, kings, courtiers, and princesses wearing pearls. The terrace was originally topped by a pavilion.

On the southern side of the terrace, which faces the Terrace of Elephants, there is access to the front wall of a terrace that was covered when the larger one was built. The four tiers of carvings here are as fresh as when first constructed.

Terrace of Elephants

The Terrace of Elephants is on a grand scale: 1,148 feet (350 m) long, it was a viewing stand for the king and the base of the great audience hall. From here the king and his court in all their magnificence and glory would view the parades of elephants, horses, chariots,

and soldiers in the Grand Square. The terrace has five outworks extending into the square; three in the center and one at each end. The middle section of the retaining wall of the terrace is decorated with life-size *garuda* and lions. Toward each end are the parades of elephants that give the terrace its name.

Around Angkor Thom are further buildings.

Ta Prohm

At Ta Prohm time has stood still. It is the nearest you will get to experiencing the wonder and awe that gripped the first European discoverers of

Angkor as they found its ruins in the jungle. That jungle has been cut back and thinned to provide access, but the larger trees remain, rising from the stones, their huge roots twisting and curling

around the stones. It is forbidden to enter the damaged galleries for fear of accidents. However, enough is accessible to give you some idea of what it must have been like. The main problem is that you are very unlikely to be left alone to enjoy any quiet reflection on the matter.

Phnom Bakheng
A favorite site from which to view Angkor Wat at sunset, Phnom Bakheng can be crowded. This was the first of the temple mountains constructed by Yasovarman I (889–910). The temple was built in accordance with Hindu cosmology.

Prasat Pravan
This is a Hindu complex with five brick towers. Built in 921, although not by royalty, and

partially restored in 1968, it is remarkable for its magnificent carvings on the inner brick walls. The central tower has two large images, that on the back wall depicting Vishnu taking the three strides with which he traversed the universe, and the other, on the right wall, of Vishnu riding a *garuda*. The northernmost tower has carvings of Vishnu's consort, Lakshmi.

Banteay Kdei and Sra Srang

Banteay Kdei is a Buddhist monastery built in the latter part of the twelfth century but never fully completed, and much of it is in ruins. It is surrounded by four concentric walls. Its four entrances are decorated with *garuda*, which hold aloft the four faces of Avalokiteshvara. Nearby and to the east of Banteay Kdei is Sra Srang (the Pool of Ablutions), a vast reservoir, constructed before the temple and decorated with *naga* heads. A small island in the middle once bore a wooden temple, of which only the base remains.

Ta Keo

This undecorated and unfinished temple, dedicated to Shiva, was built by Jayavarman V (968–1001). The temple mountain is crowned by a 164-foot (50-m) tower, which is surrounded by four lesser towers at each corner of the upper platform. Even without the decoration that it would clearly have had if completed, it is an impressive structure and the first at Angkor that was built entirely of sandstone.

Thommanon

Dedicated to Shiva and Vishnu, this temple underwent extensive restoration in the 1960s.

Preah Khan

One of the largest complexes at Angkor, Preah Khan bears comparison with Ta Prohm, and has the same maze of corridors, enclosures, and towers, but has been better preserved. Built by Jayavarman VII, it was dedicated in 1191 to 515 divinities and was a major center of worship, with eighteen major festivals taking place each year. The whole complex covers a large area. The temple itself is surrounded by a long wall approached by four processional walkways flanked by balustrades representing the Churning of the Sea of Milk; many of the figures are headless. Four vaulted corridors enter the central sanctuary from the four cardinal points. Many finely carved images remain, including those of *apsaras* and *essais* (sages). Entry is from the west gate. Look out for the Grecian-looking two-story building inside the east gate, which remains something of a mystery.

Banteay Srei

Dedicated to Shiva, Banteay Srei (Citadel of Women) is the most delicate and beautiful of the temples at Angkor. Built of pinkish stone, the carving is as fine and delicate as any to be found anywhere. Construction began in 967 and was commissioned by a Brahman who may have been a tutor to Jayavarman V. The building is square and is approached from the east by a causeway. The carvings represent male and female deities and scenes from the Hindu epic *Ramayana*. Almost every surface of the interior is covered with decoration. This is one temple that must be seen in order to view Khmer art at its finest and most beautiful.

chapter eight

BUSINESS BRIEFING

GOVERNMENT POLICY

Cambodia's economy is growing, though it is still hampered by the effects of the years of conflict and the policies of the Pol Pot regime. Banking and

financial structures are being reformed and developed; much has been done to restore and improve the country's basic infrastructure; the port of Sihanoukville has been enlarged and modernized; and there are plans to develop rail links with ASEAN neighbors. Cambodia has received injections of aid and investment from international sources. Its textile industry has been a success, though it is now facing tougher competition, and there are promising developments in the mining and oil sectors. The construction sector has also done well in recent years.

The Cambodian government actively encourages foreign enterprise and investment, and companies and firms with well-thought-through proposals are welcomed. Any proposals should emphasize the benefits to Cambodia. The government is anxious to improve the education and skills of the population, so reference to training schemes to develop skills among your Cambodian management and workforce will be welcomed. Moreover, it will assist your project if you acquire local representatives or partners to help manage things on your behalf. There are good practical reasons for doing so, associated with the way Cambodians do business.

Nongovernmental Organizations (NGOs) play a significant role in Cambodia's recovery and development by channeling foreign aid into sectors such as education, medical and health services, welfare programs, assisting small businesses, and tackling social problems. They provide employment, expertise, and training, and aim at increasing Cambodia's own self-sufficiency and ability to sustain improved standards of living. NGOs can be criticized for developing a culture of dependency or for lack of awareness of the people's own desires, but they represent a relatively  efficient and cost-effective use of aid while providing training and employment.

BUSINESS CULTURE

Business in Cambodia is based on those same core Asian values underpinning the business cultures of its neighbors, namely family, respect, hierarchy, networking, consensus, and nonconfrontation. In such a culture personal contacts are important, and the higher up the hierarchy these are the more influential they will be. If you are planning to do business in Cambodia or with Cambodians, try to establish personal contact with someone who can introduce you to the people you will need to see in government and business circles. It may not be possible to see the minister concerned: large international companies have access to such people through their own links or by virtue of their reputation. In that sense they have "rank"; but if you represent a smaller enterprise and have no existing personal contact, approach the Cambodian embassy or trade mission in your own country in order to get an introduction to someone who can assist you. Don't arrive in Cambodia to do business without having a local contact. There are Web sites providing information and offering assistance, and the Cambodian government has its own site.

If you are assigned to Cambodia to work in an enterprise that is already established, your own status will depend on your position in the hierarchy. You will become aware that interaction between yourself and Cambodian colleagues and staff within the office will be more formal than you are accustomed to, although younger people with some Western experience may be more relaxed. It is important to find out the ages and positions held of the people you are working with so that you may treat them with the appropriate respect.

Watch the Time

To avoid confusion about time, use the twenty-four-hour clock for making appointments and arranging meetings. When writing dates, Cambodians use the system common throughout the region of day/month/year: 14/4/2009 for April 14, 2009. To avoid confusion it is advisable to use the full date in correspondence, and to reconfirm meetings and appointments, if possible, in advance.

OFFICE ETIQUETTE AND PROTOCOL

If you are employed in an office you will, as a foreigner, be likely to be in a position of some authority, although, depending on the type of business and its size, you may have Cambodians in positions higher in the hierarchy. Within the office, it is important to show respect to those senior to yourself and also to those who are senior in years. Any differences of opinion or any criticism must be conveyed in indirect and respectful terms. Similarly, you can expect respectful behavior from those below you in the corporate structure, but in return treat them with consideration and respect. If there are failings, deal with them diplomatically and not in public. Confrontation would be counterproductive, and it is you who would lose face and respect.

MANAGEMENT STYLE

Management in the private sector has been influenced by French corporate structures. There is usually a director general, followed by a general manager, and then managers. Occasionally, a president may rank above the director general. You will have a position in this hierarchy, and should recognize the responsibilities you have to those above and below you in the hierarchy. Remember that, whatever the managerial structure of the business and the office, a confrontational approach will be self-defeating, as mentioned above. However, you are entitled to the respect of those below you in the management structure and those younger in years, and can tactfully indicate that you expect it.

BUSINESS CARDS

Carry enough business cards to hand to all present, beginning with the most senior member of the group. If possible have your card printed in Khmer on one side and English on the other. Offer the card with both hands, or the right hand. If the card is printed in Khmer, present it with that side up. When offered a card accept it with both hands or the right hand and a slight inclination of the head. The way you treat the card is indicative of your respect for the person presenting it.

MEETINGS AND GREETINGS

You will encounter a mixture of traditional and Western behavior. Cambodians traditionally greet each other by placing the palms of the hands together and raised to the chest, and bowing slightly. You may still see such greetings at meetings and conferences, particularly among older participants or when a younger person meets an older. However, the Western handshake has become the usual practice between men, although women usually continue to exchange the traditional greeting between themselves. Foreigners should shake the hands of both men and women, although you should wait until the woman extends her hand before extending your own. If she does not, a slight bow will show courtesy and respect.

On a first meeting with Cambodians with whom you may be conducting business, greet the highest-ranking person first. If you are in a group, the most senior member of your group should greet the most senior member of the other. Other members should be introduced in hierarchical order and using any titles that indicate academic achievement (such as "Doctor," for instance) and their position in your organization or delegation (chairman, project manager, personal assistant), so that both sides understand the levels of authority. When addressing your Cambodian counterparts, use their titles until you are informed otherwise. If you have not noted their titles and rank in previous written information sent to you, their business cards will contain that information.

It is not polite to get straight down to business. Meetings should begin with casual conversation —about your journey to the meeting, recent events, your impressions of the country, and so on. Keep your remarks favorable and uncritical. You may be offered some tea, a soft drink, or water. It is polite to take a few sips, but not necessary to drink it all. If you do it is likely to be refilled. This preamble is to enable everyone to size each other up and to form first impressions.

A meeting will have been set up for a particular length of time. Ascertain what time has been allocated for it, especially if dealing with a person in the government or bureaucracy, but also if with a business contact. Your Cambodian counterpart will be reluctant to take the initiative to end the meeting, as that would be bad manners. As the guest you should make the move when the time allocated has ended.

NEGOTIATIONS

As the meeting and business discussions develop, be polite, and be careful to avoid confrontation. Agreement may not be reached, but differences can be made clear without creating conflict, as face-saving is important for both sides. Proposals from the Cambodian side will be cautiously worded and put forward as suggestions, while silence is an indication of disagreement, which will not be openly stated. Negotiations, therefore, take the form of probing by both sides to arrive at a consensus.

The negotiation process is not merely a matter of language. Cambodians conceal anger and frustration, often behind a smile that may indicate incomprehension, disagreement, nervousness, or irritation. Also bear in mind that your counterpart may not be able to commit to any decision at the time of your meeting, but may have to report progress to a superior.

The Cambodian approach may appear frustrating, time-wasting, and indecisive, but speaking frankly and forcibly, being bombastic and boastful, or expressing frustration and anger will be counterproductive. From the Cambodian perspective, you will have lost face and also their respect for what they consider bad manners and lack of control.

Younger colleagues and subordinates who have been trained overseas are likely to fall in with Western management styles more easily than people without such training and experience. On the other hand, the latter are likely to have knowledge and understanding of and links into the bureaucracy and existing management systems. Their advice and experience should be treated with respect, and any changes introduced with regard for their views and feelings.

SPEECHES AND PRESENTATIONS

The basic organization of an event where you may need to give a speech or presentation will be much as you are used to. In most cases you will have access to familiar audiovisual and computer-assisted programs. PowerPoint presentations with the employment of visual images, charts, diagrams, and graphs can help an audience, not all of whom may be fluent in English, to understand you. However, the situation will be formal and people mentioned in the presentation or spoken to from the platform should be addressed according to title and rank. Such public events are often arranged to present a consensus arrived at beforehand through negotiations with interested parties and their intermediaries, and no one should be seen to lose face.

If you are delivering your speech or presentation in English to an audience containing people not fully conversant with the language, you should speak clearly and slowly, avoiding jargon, and explain concepts clearly.

Interpreters

If necessary, employ an interpreter. If you are presenting concepts, information, and views that may be challenged, or that may affect the interests of members of the audience, it would be wise to employ your own interpreter rather than one supplied by an organization with its own agenda.

Remember to concentrate on those you are addressing—you should avoid the temptation to turn to or to address the interpreter. However, also avoid prolonged eye contact, as it may be interpreted as aggressive.

BUREAUCRACY AND CORRUPTION

Although they operate like private enterprises, most modern Cambodian businesses are public entities. Each province in the country is governed by a local political leader, and corruption is widespread, particularly in the public sector. Access to timber concessions is one area where corruption has been rife, but there are other segments of the economy where individual enterprises benefit from their connections with government officials. Cambodia received a low ranking from Transparency International in 2006 and in that same year the World Bank froze payments for programs said to involve corrupt practices by government officials. The government is attempting to tackle the problem, but it reaches down through society to the lower levels of the bureaucracy and public life.

Because of the emphasis on personal dealings within business relationships, it is necessary to ascertain, as far as possible, the status and connections of those with whom you are hoping to do business. Be wary of those who would place you under an obligation by proffering lavish gifts and hospitality. If you are offered such hospitality or gifts, either politely decline or reciprocate to an equal degree, and thus retain your status.

GIFT GIVING

Always a sensitive issue, gift giving is not obligatory, although, when visiting a representative of another firm for the first time, you may wish to present a gift of small value bearing your company logo, or a sample of your product, or something typical of your own country. Seek advice from more experienced colleagues or from your local partner or agent. If you are invited to a celebration relating to a member of office staff or hierarchy or their family, again seek advice from your colleagues. The fundamental rule is to avoid incurring obligations that you cannot expect to meet in a manner you are comfortable with.

Remember that potential recipients may have religious prohibitions regarding alcohol or certain food products. It is advisable to make yourself aware of the religious affiliations and possible sensitivities of all potential recipients. This is an area in which the advice of an experienced secretary or personal assistant can be invaluable.

WOMEN IN BUSINESS

Although there are very few women holding responsible positions in government, they are important in the business sector. Most small  businesses and privately owned shops are staffed by women. Most large firms employ female office staff and secretaries, some of whom attain important executive positions, although the higher levels of management are exclusively male. Nevertheless, remember that secretaries are often repositories of knowledge, both business-related and personal. Your personal secretary can advise on matters of etiquette, intra- and interdepartmental relations, and personal foibles, and offer an understanding of the workings of the business and its management.

WORKING WITHIN THE SYSTEM

Working or conducting business in Cambodia requires patience and understanding of the traditions and practices that affect relations within the workplace, between business contacts, and between those business contacts and government officials. However, Cambodians are moving away from the trauma of recent years and as the economy modernizes and expands, and business and commercial opportunities and contacts grow, relations become easier. Nevertheless, the underlying culture remains and it is wise to conform to it until you are sure of your position in it.

BLESSING THE PROJECT

When a project is begun, or a new building or a new office is opened, your Cambodian colleagues may suggest that it should be blessed in a ceremony conducted by monks. The ceremony requires sitting on the floor while the monks seated opposite chant and say prayers, after which they are ceremoniously fed. The whole event may last for over two hours, during which you must be seated in the lotus position or with your legs tucked to one side. To ease the discomfort it may be possible to have a low platform constructed upon which the monks may sit at a higher level so that you may at least have a cushion without raising your head above theirs. It may also be suggested that the new building should have a spirit house, in which case seek the advice of your Cambodian colleagues.

Sitting Pretty

At a blessing service such as that described above, a European guest watched what his Cambodian friends were doing and sat on the floor in the lotus position. As the service went on his calves cramped, but he refused to change position, not wishing to attract attention to himself or to cause offense. Fortunately the service was relatively short, but by the time it ended and he had endured agony of body and mind, he found that his legs had locked and he could not get up. It required a period of equally agonizing massage before he regained mobility.

chapter nine

COMMUNICATING

LANGUAGE

Khmer is the official language of Cambodia, but English and French are also spoken by educated people. English is increasingly important in business, and the majority of those with whom you work will have some command of it—often a very good command—and will usually be happy to use it. French is a useful subsidiary language that many older Khmers will have learned.

Speaking English

Cambodians have not been slow to recognize the advantages of learning English. English is the language of tourism and of commerce and English language schools and classes operate in all kinds of locales. Many of the teachers may not themselves be fluent in English, but the demand is there. You will find that many of the Cambodians you meet will be anxious to try out their stumbling English on you, rather than have you try out your stumbling Khmer on them.

Khmer

It would be polite and diplomatic for the visitor to learn the basic pleasantries in Khmer. Although the traditional script will be unfamiliar and indecipherable to most people, the language is also transcribed into Roman script, and this makes it possible to learn some of the words. Nobody will expect fluency, but your efforts will be appreciated. If you learn more, note that

there are dialects throughout the country, so you are likely to encounter difficulties when traveling.

Khmer has its roots in Sanskrit and Pali, and has been influenced by contacts with the languages of its neighbors and, during the colonial period, by French, which introduced many technical and medical terms. Unlike the languages of its neighbors, Khmer is nontonal, but it has a complex system of thirty-three consonants and twenty-three vowels. Transliteration into the Roman alphabet under French rule means that this does not assist the accurate pronunciation of Khmer words by English-speakers. However, although the pronunciation is difficult, the grammar is simple, as there are no verb conjugations and no different endings for singular, plural, masculine, or feminine nouns. Changes in tense are conveyed by adding a few words. Transliteration into English is difficult, and you will find different transliterations occurring in different Khmer language guides.

> ### *FORMS OF ADDRESS*
> Social standing and politeness govern
> Cambodian society, and it is important to use
> the correct forms of address based on age and
> social position. As a foreigner you will be
> forgiven for not knowing all the requisite forms
> of address, but the following advice may help
> avoid embarrassment.
>
> *Niak* (you) may be used in most situations and
> with either sex.
>
> *Lok* (Mister) may be used for men of your own
> age or older.
>
> *Lok srei* (Madam) is a formal address for
> women of your age or older.
>
> *Bang srei* (older sister) may be used for less
> formal occasions.
>
> *Bang* is a convenient neutral pronoun for men or
> women who are, or appear to be, older than you.
>
> *Koat* is the respectful form of the third person
> singular or plural for men or women. The
> common form is *ke.*

If you stay in the country long enough to make
close friends, you may be invited to use the family-
oriented forms of address mentioned in Chapter 2.
Until then, err on the side of formality and respect.

FACE-TO-FACE

Cambodians should be addressed with the respect
their position and age call for. Face should be

maintained, and no public humiliation caused. On the other hand, you yourself will be told what the person speaking to you believes you want to hear. Be attentive to nuances of voice and behavior; but the true situation may be revealed only by intermediaries, and only then probably in guarded terms.

In conversation, be sure to speak clearly and to avoid colloquialisms and slang with which nonnative English speakers will be unfamiliar. Many Cambodians can speak English fluently, but others will be less confident and liable to mishear or misunderstand. Conversely, you may take time to accustom yourself to the nuances of Cambodian spoken English. If you need to ask someone to repeat a statement, do so politely, perhaps with some deprecatory remark about your hearing or understanding. In time you will become accustomed to Cambodian pronunciation and grammatical foibles.

HUMOR

Cambodians possess a sense of humor and respond to the ridiculous. Slapstick comedy is popular on TV or on the stage, but refrain from laughing at people in difficulty or who make a mistake in real life. If comic action takes place in a theatrical performance, the audience will respond; but in personal relations remember that face must be saved and that there is a fine line between what is humorous and what produces shame. At times, too, a laugh or smile may be an indication that a person has not fully understood what you have said and is an attempt to cover embarrassment. On the other hand, as a foreigner you will make mistakes that are humorous. Your Cambodian acquaintances will be too polite to laugh or comment, but if you can laugh or smile at your own errors, they will be delighted that you are not embarrassed and will laugh or smile with you.

BODY LANGUAGE

Body language is important, especially when verbal communication may be difficult. A hearty manner will be regarded as offensive, and the perpetrator as boorish and rude. Your posture and demeanor should indicate respect and reserve. How you sit or stand may convey respect and dignity, or aggression and plain bad manners. Thus you should not stand with one or both hands in your pockets or on your hips, as this indicates disrespect and arrogance. However, to clasp them lightly in front of you shows respect. When sitting, it is disrespectful to lean back with legs outstretched or to sit with them crossed or parted. To pat a person on the back is a sign of disrespect, especially if that person is older or in a senior position.

To point at someone is considered rude, and to jab a finger at someone while making a point in an argument would be considered offensive. If it is necessary to catch someone's attention, or summon them, use the whole hand with the palm turned down. To summon with the finger and the palm turned up is an offensive gesture. If it is necessary to point, use the thumb only.

Facial gestures such as grimacing, pouting, and winking are also considered impolite, and should be avoided in any formal setting.

These general rules of conduct may appear relatively insignificant, but in a society and a business world where age and seniority carry respect, they can make a great difference to how one is perceived. If you develop good relations with Cambodians, then the formality may be relaxed, especially in private, but in the business environment and in public it is necessary to show respect and to save face. Remember that Western society once had similar codes of behavior, and courtesy was regarded as important.

Take No Chances

It had been a successful meeting for the Australian representative of a firm seeking an agreement with his Cambodian counterpart. As it ended, and people began to leave the room, the Australian came alongside the leader of the Cambodian group, gave him a friendly slap on the back, and wished him well. Disconcerted, the Cambodian gave a slight nod and made no further comment. The Australian received no follow-up, and the deal was not concluded.

SERVICES
Telephone
Cell phones are the main means of telephonic communication, and are ubiquitous. Although the landline system, severely damaged during the years of conflict, has been largely restored, calls between the provinces are cheaper by cell phone. Traditional public pay phones may still be found in the cities, but privately operated roadside booths, where the operators have mobile phones and have leased lines to offer a domestic service, are found everywhere. International calls may be made from card phones and prepaid cards are available. Internet phoning is also relatively cheap. The Cambodian country code is +855

E-mail
Cambodia's Internet domain is .kh. Internet cafés provide cheap access to the Internet, and will also send faxes. However, some may have outdated equipment and slow connections. Many medium-range hotels have business centers that provide Internet services at a reasonable price. Those in the top-end hotels are much more expensive.

Mail
Each town has a post office; there are five in Phnom Penh. All provide a mailbox service. The mail is reasonably reliable, but you may prefer to send important or valuable items by one of the international courier services, which have offices in Phnom Penh, and some also in Siem Reap. If you

send mail over the counter at a post office, ensure that the items are franked before you leave.

THE MEDIA
Many Cambodian newspapers and private television and radio stations rely on support from political parties. Press freedom is not guaranteed, but the government has expressed support for a free press and media.

Newspapers
The main newspapers are *Cambodia Daily* and *Phnom Penh Post* (English-language); and *Reaksmei Kampuchea* and *Kaoh Santepheap* (both pro-government dailies). The news agency is Agence Kampuchea Presse (AKP).

Radio and Television
The state radio broadcaster is the National Radio of Cambodia. Phnom Penh Radio, a commercial station run jointly with the Phnom Penh municipality, is the county's most popular station. Other commercial stations are operated by Apsara Radio and TV and Bayon Radio and TV.

The BBC, Radio Australia, and Radio France Internationale are available in and around Phnom Penh, as is Radio Love—an English-language Western pop music station.

There are nine television channels, including two relay stations with French and Vietnamese broadcasts. National Television of Cambodia

(TVK) is the state broadcaster. Commercial and private channels are TV3, jointly run with the Phnom Penh municipality, Apsara TV, TV5, CTN, Bayon TV, and CTV9. There are also eighteen regional relay stations. There is no restriction on the ownership of satellite dishes.

CONCLUSION

Cambodia has passed through a long and, at times, tumultuous history, overshadowed by the terrible events that took place between 1975 and 1979 under the ruthless regime of Pol Pot and the Khmer Rouge. The experiences of these years live on in memories and monuments.

Proud of their ancient culture and long traditions, and anxious to retain their sense of identity, the Cambodian people have rebuilt their country with strength and determination, to take its place in the world as a modern nation. Cambodia welcomes visitors with all the warmth, charm, and hospitality that its people naturally possess in abundance.

Appendix: Useful Words and Phrases

There is no commonly accepted form of transliteration from Khmer—with its thirty-three consonants and twenty-three vowels—into English, and publications on Cambodia vary. The following transliterations are kept as simple as possible in order to produce spoken sounds that a Cambodian might understand.

Hello	*Chum reeup sooa*
Good-bye	*Chum reeup lear* (formal)
	Lear hauwee (informal)
Please	*Sohm*
Thank you	*Aw kohn*
Excuse me / I'm sorry	*Sohm toh*
Yes	*Baat* (used by men)
	Jaas (used by women)
No	*Tay*
I	*K'nyom*
You	*Niak*
I don't understand	*K'nyom s'dap men baan*
Can you speak English?	*Niak jehs nit-yaly par sar Onglai?*
Lavatory	*Bong-kun*
Where is…?	*…. now ain nar?*
Come	*Mow*
Go	*Toa*
What is your … ?	*Niak . . . ai?*
What is your name?	*Niak ch-moo-ah ai?*
Where are you going?	*Tow nar?*
I am going to …	*K'nyom tow …*
I want to go to …	*K'nyom chong tow …*
Where is the … ?	*… now ai nar?*
I am not well	*K'nyom men su-rooel kloo un tay*
I am lost	*K'nom vung-veing plaow*
How much does it cost?	*Telai pon maan?*
Very expensive	*Telai nahs*
What is your best price?	*Dait pon maan?*

Morning	*Pel pruk*
Noon	*T'ngai terong*
Afternoon	*Pel rohsiel*
Evening	*Pel l'ingiat*
Night	*Pel yop*
Day	*T'ingai*
Today	*T'ingai nee*
Tomorrow	*T'ingai sa-ait*
Yesterday	*M'sell-mine*
Hour	*Maung*
What is the time?	*Maung pon maan?*

Numerals

0	*sohn*
1	*moi*
2	*pee*
3	*bei*
4	*boun*
5	*bram*
6	*bram-moi*
7	*bram-pee*
8	*bram-bei*
9	*bram-boun*
10	*duop*
11	*duop-moi*
12	*duop-pee*

Some words have been adopted into Khmer from French or English, for example *pohs poli*, (police station), *ohtel* (hotel), *taksee* (taxi), and *restoran* (restaurant).

Further Reading

Chandler, David P. *A History of Cambodia*. Chiang Mai, Thailand: 1998; Boulder, Colorado; and Oxford: Westview Press, 2000.

Chandler, David P. *Brother Number One: A Political Biography of Pol Pot*. Chiang Mai, Thailand: Silkworm Books, 1999.

Jessup, Helen. *Art and Architecture in Cambodia*. London: Thames & Hudson, 1994.

Kiernan, Ben, and Chanthou Boua. *Peasants and Politics in Kampuchea 1942-1981*. London: Zed; New York: Sharpe, 1982.

Lewis, Norman. *A Dragon Apparent: Travels in Cambodia, Laos and Vietnam*. 1951. New York: Scribner, and London: Jonathan Cape, 1951.

Livingstone, Carol. *Gecko Tails. A Journey Through Cambodia*. London: Weidenfeld & Nicolson, 1996.

Osborne, Lewis. *Sihanouk. Prince of Light, Peace of Darkness*. St. Leonards: Allen & Unwin, 1994.

Philpotts, Robert. *The Coast of Cambodia*. London: Blackwater Books, 2001.

Ponchaud, Francois. *Cambodia Year Zero*, Harmondsworth: Penguin, 1978.

Pym, Christopher (ed.) (abridged). *Henri Mouhot's Diary, Travels in the Central Plains of Siam, Cambodia and Laos During the Years 1858-61*. Kuala Lumpur: Oxford University Press, 1966.

Ray, Nick. *Cambodia*. Hawthorn, Victoria; Oakland, California; London; and Paris: Lonely Planet Publications, 2005.

Shawcross, William. *The Quality of Mercy: Cambodia, Holocaust, and Modern Conscience*. New York: Simon and Schuster, 1984.

Szymusiak, Molyda (trans. Linda Coverdale). *The Stones Cry Out. A Cambodian Childhood, 1975-80*. London: Jonathan Cape, 1987.

Vickery, Michael. *Cambodia, 1975-1882*. Sydney: Allen & Unwin in association with Southend Press, 1984.

culture smart! cambodia

Index

age structure 10, 16
air travel 106–7, 111
alcohol 86, 99, 151
Angkor 8, 16, 18–21, 24, 49, 52, 90, 91, 103, 116, 117, 121–30, 133, 137, 138
Angkor Thom 20–21, 123, 130–31, 135
Angkor Wat 22–3, 57, 124–30, 136
animism 11, 17, 54–5
Annam (central Vietnam) 21
antiques 101–2
Asian neighbors, attitudes to 49
Association of Southeast Asian Nations (ASEAN) 31–2, 37, 49, 110, 140

Bana (demon king) 129
Banteay Kdei 137
Banteay Srei 138–9
bargaining 79, 101
Battambang 10, 24, 25, 109, 110, 111
Bayon 131–4
bicycles 108, 123
birth 59–60
blessing the project 152–3
boat travel 110–11
body language 158–9
Bokor National Park 120
Bon Om Tuk 57–8, 93
Buddhism 17, 19, 40, 41, 54, 59, 64, 65
    Mahayana 20
    Theravada (Hinayana) 11, 15, 20, 52–3
bureaucracy 148, 150
buses 107, 109–10
business cards 72, 144–5, 146
business culture 142–3

cafés 90, 98
calendar 55
Cambodian People's National Liberation Armed Forces 28
Cambodian People's Party (CPP) 33, 34
cars 107–9, 122–3
Chams, the 16, 20, 21, 50, 53, 57, 94, 121, 130, 132, 133, 134
character 9, 51, 162
Chat Preah Nenkal (Royal Plowing Festival) 56
Chaul Chnam (Khmer New Year) 56
Chaul Chnam Chen (Lunar New Year) 55–6
Chenla 17–18
children 81–2

China 9, 27, 31
Chinese 10, 15, 16, 45, 50, 55, 56
chopsticks 72, 85
Christianity 11, 54
climate 10, 14–15
clothing
    buying 105
    see also dress
Coalition Government of Democratic Kapuchea 32
Cochin-China (southern Vietnam) 21
Communism, Communists 25, 30, 41
consensus 42
constitution 33–4, 82–3
corruption 27, 149–50
crime 116
culture, traditional 90–92
currency 11, 36
cyclos 123

daily life and routine 76–9
dance 90, 91
death 59, 64–5
Democratic Party 26
dress 55–6, 68–9, 92
drinks 71, 86, 87, 96–7, 146

Eastern Highlands 13–14
eating 72, 85
eating out 97–9
economy 34–8, 140
education 82–4
elephant rides 123
entertaining 84–7
environment 13–14
ethnic makeup 10
etiquette 69–73, 143–4
eye contact 149

face, maintaining 156–7
family 44–7, 73, 79–82
festivals and national celebrations 55–8
food 84–7, 94–6, 151
foreigners, attitudes to 48–9
forms of address 156
French rule 8–9, 15, 21, 24, 25, 26, 54, 96, 118
Funan 17

Geneva Conference (1954) 26
gifts 55, 64, 70, 150–51
government 11, 38–9
    policy 140–41
greetings 66–7, 145–6
group identity 42

handshake 67, 145
hats 70–71
health and medical care 112–15
Heng Samrin 31
hierarchy 41–2, 143, 145–6, 150
Hinduism, Hindus 17, 19, 20, 40, 41, 52, 54, 125, 132, 136
history 17–34
    early kingdoms 17–18
    the Khmer Empire 18–19
    the rise of Theravada Buddhism 20
    the decline of the Khmers 20–21
    French control 24
    Japanese occupation 25
        guerrilla war and independence 25–7
    the Cambodian civil war 27
    the overthrow of Sihanouk 27–8
    rise of the Khmer Rouge 29
    the reign of terror 30–31
    Vietnamese invasion 31–2
    ceasefire and the UN peace process 32–3
    the new constitution 33–4
Ho Chi Minh trail 27
hotels 97, 99, 102, 160
household help 88–9
housing 74–6
humor 157–8
Hun Sen 33, 34, 39

independence 9, 26
India 9, 19, 52, 91
Indochina 22, 24, 26
Indravarman I 18–19
International Conference on Cambodia (1991) 32
invitations 69–73
Islam/Muslims 11, 16, 50, 53

Japanese occupation 9, 25
Jayavarman II 18
Jayavarman V 137, 138
Jayavarman VII 20–21, 57, 93–4, 131, 138

Kampong Cham 10, 16, 104, 109, 111
Kampong Saom *see* Sihanoukville
Kampong Thom 10, 119
Kampot 10, 109, 110
Kampuchean United Front for National Salvation 31
Khieu Samphan 29
Khmer empire 8, 18–19, 117
Khmer Issarak (Free Khmer) 25–6
Khmer Loeu (Chuenchet) 16, 50–51, 54

Khmer National Armed Forces (FANK) 28
Khmer Rouge 8, 9, 15, 16, 28–33, 35, 44, 48, 50, 53, 54, 60, 82, 90, 94, 117, 119, 162
Khmers 8, 10, 15, 16, 18, 20–21, 25, 26, 45–6, 50, 64, 65, 79, 127, 132, 133–4, 154
"Killing Fields" (Choeung Ek) 8, 49, 119
Kirirom National Park 120
Kratie 111
Krishna (Hindu deity) 129

language 9, 11, 15, 16, 20, 48, 84, 86, 98–9, 157
    Khmer 155
    speaking English 154
    useful words and phrases 163–4
Laos 8, 12, 21, 107
Lon Nol, General 28, 29, 30, 50

malaria 114
management style 144
Marinara (a deity) 19, 52
markets 78, 79, 101, 104, 105
marriage 59, 61–4
meals 84–6, 87
Mekong River 12, 14, 17, 58, 111
minibuses 110, 122
minorities, attitudes to 50–51
Monivong, King 24
motorcycles (*motos*) 107, 108, 109, 123
Mouhot, Henri 22–3
museums 49
music 64, 65, 90, 91–2

National United Front for an Independent, Neutral, Peaceful and Cooperative Cambodia (FUNCINPEC) 33, 34, 36
Neang Neak 62
negotiations 147–8
nightlife 99–100, 118
Nongovernmental Organizations (NGOs) 141
Norodom, King 21, 24
Norodom Suramarit, King 26
North Vietnam 29
North Vietnamese 27, 28, 29

pagodas 92
paintings 102–3
P'chun Ben 57
pedicabs 123
pedlos 108
People's Republic of Kampuchea (PRK) 31, 35, 82
People's Socialist Community (Sangkum Reastr Niyum) 26

Phnom Bakheng 136
Phnom Penh (main references) 12, 117–18
Phnom Sontuk 119
places to visit 116–39
Pol Pot (Saloth Sar) 9, 15, 29, 31, 34, 140, 162
politeness and manners 42–4, 143–4
Prasat Pravan 136–7
Preah Khan 138
Preah Tong 61–2
presentations 148
public holidays 58

rabies 115
radio 92, 161
rail travel 110
Rainsy, Sam 34
Ranariddh, Prince 32, 33
religion 11, 17, 19, 40–41, 47, 52–5
remorque-motos 123
respect 41, 48, 67, 81, 92, 143–4, 148, 156, 159
restaurants 64, 69, 85–6, 87, 90, 97, 98, 99
rites of passage 59–65
road travel 107–9

safety 115–16
sculpture 103
Second World War 9, 25
self-control 42
Shiva (Hindu deity) 19, 52, 129, 137, 138
shoe removal 70, 92
shopping 77–8
   for pleasure 100–105
Siem Reap (main references) 10, 121
Sihamoni, King Norodom 34, 38
Sihanouk, King 9, 25–34
Sihanoukville (Kampong Saom) 10, 98, 99, 110, 118, 140
silver 103
Sisophon 10, 24
Sisowath, King 24, 28
social behavior 66, 68
som pas 66–7, 69
South Vietnam 26, 27, 28
Soviet Union 31
speeches 148–9
Sra Srang 137
Suryavarman II, King 124, 127

Ta Keo 137
Ta Prohm 135–6, 138

table manners 84, 85
Takeo 10, 104, 109, 110
taxis 107, 108–9
tea 71, 86, 87, 96, 146
television 11, 51, 92, 161–2
Terrace of Elephants 135
Terrace of the Leper King 134–5
textiles 103–4, 140
Thailand 8, 12, 21, 24, 25, 26, 91, 107
Thais 8, 18, 20, 21, 25, 49, 50, 121, 127
Theravada (Hinayana) Buddhism 11, 15, 20, 52–3
Thommanon 138
time 11, 143
   attitudes to 47–8
tipping 99
Tonkin (northern Vietnam) 21
Tonle Sap Lake 12, 14, 16, 18, 21, 34, 57, 111
Tonle Sap River 12, 57, 58, 94
tourism 9, 37, 48, 51, 99, 100, 101, 106, 116, 121

unexploded ordnance 115–16
United Nations 32, 34, 36, 51
United Nations Security Counc
United Nations Transitional Authority in Cambodia (UNTAC) 32, 36, 39, 51
United States 26, 27, 28, 35, 36

Vichy government (Paris) 25
Viet Minh 25
Vietcong 27, 28, 29
Vietnam 9, 12, 20, 21, 25, 26, 27, 32, 107
Vietnamese 8, 10, 15–16, 20, 31, 45, 49, 50, 53, 55, 56
Visaka Puja 56–7
Vishnu (Hindu deity) 19, 52, 124, 125, 126, 129, 137, 138

water, drinking 71, 96, 97, 146
wats (monasteries) 92, 118
wildlife 14
women
   and bars/clubs 99–100
   in business 151
   in the family 80–81
wood carving 104
working within the system 152

Yasovarman I 19, 136

Acknowledgment

This book is dedicated to my wife, Anne.